A Truant Disposition

Discovering the Tragedy of Hamlet
through the Role of Horatio

Revised Second Edition

Carol J. Grieb

INFINITY
PUBLISHING

ISBN 978-1-4958-1075-6

Published April 2018

INFINITY PUBLISHING
1094 New DeHaven Street, Suite 100
West Conshohocken, PA 19428-2713
Toll-free (877) BUY BOOK
Local Phone (610) 941-9999
Fax (610) 941-9959
Info@buybooksontheweb.com
www.buybooksontheweb.com

To Chelley

ACKNOWLEDGMENTS

T his book was written with encouragement from my sister, Chelley D. Gardner-Smith. After viewing Kenneth Branagh's film, *Hamlet*,[1] the following interpretation of the play was researched and developed. My understanding of *Hamlet* is largely indebted to Branagh's superb efforts to include rather than dismiss characters and passages from the early texts of Shakespeare's *Hamlet*.

This edition includes corrections and additions to previous printings.

Author photo is courtesy of Mel Mougin. Cover design is by the author.

I am grateful for research assistance from the University of Kansas Libraries and the University of Missouri-Kansas City Libraries.

I am also grateful for the guidance offered by Chelley Gardner-Smith, Andrea Zuercher, Maureen Godman, Cheryl Burbach, Christopher Crouse-Dick, Mark Luce, and Janet Majure.

I especially thank teachers, friends, and family.

---

[1]   Kenneth Branagh, director, *Hamlet*, (West Hollywood: Castle Rock Entertainment, 1996), Film.

CONTENTS

THE EARLIEST FORM OF PRINTING PRESS

Robert Hoe, *A Short History of the Printing Press* (New York: R. Hoe 1902), 6.

PREFACE

For William Shakespeare's *The Tragedy of Hamlet, Prince of Denmark,* I referred to the early text sources, First Quarto (Q1[2]), Second Quarto (Q2[3]) and First Folio (F1[4]).

The Three-Text Hamlet (Kliman & Bertram) was the primary reference.[5] Act and scene references generally follow Ann Thompson and Neil Taylor's *The Arden Shakespeare "Hamlet,"* third series.[6]

Pointed textual references to acts and scenes are written out (example: Act 4, scene 3). Parenthetical references to acts are shown with a capital roman numeral, the scene follows with a small roman numeral (example: IV.iii.). Line numbers are generally not listed. Where line numbers are used, they follow line numbers in *The Arden Shakespeare "Hamlet,"* third series (Thompson and Taylor).

---

[2] From the title-page of Q1: *THE Tragicall Historie of HAMLET Prince of Denmarke,* By William Shake-speare. As it hath beene diuerse times acted by his Highnesse seruants in the Cittie of London: as also in the two Vniuersities of Cambridge and Oxford, and elsewhere ... At London printed for N. L. and Iohn Trundell. 1603.

[3] From the title-page of Q2: *THE Tragicall Historie of HAMLET, Prince of Denmarke.* By William Shakespeare. Newly imprinted and enlarged to almost as much againe as it was, according to the true and perfect Coppie. ... AT LONDON, Printed by I. R. for N. L. ... 1604.

[4] From the title-page of F1: *MR. WILLIAM SHAKESPEARES COMEDIES, HISTORIES, & TRAGEDIES.* Published according to the True Originall Copies. LONDON / Printed by Isaac Iaggard, and Ed. Blount. 1623.

[5] Bernice W. Kliman and Paul Bertram, eds., *The Three-Text Hamlet: Parallel Texts of the First and Second Quartos and First Folio,* 2nd ed. (New York: AMS Press, 2003).

[6] Ann Thompson and Neil Taylor, eds., *The Arden Shakespeare "Hamlet,"* 3rd ser. (London: Thomson Learning, 2007).

Following are additional annotated sources for the play's texts:

Ann Thompson and Neil Taylor, eds., *The Arden Shakespeare "Hamlet,"* 3rd ser., Rev. ed. (London: Bloomsbury Arden Shakespeare, 2016).

Edward Hubler and Sylvan Barnet, eds., *The Tragedy of Hamlet, Prince of Denmark,* by William Shakespeare (New York: Signet Classics, Penguin, 1987).

Harold Jenkins, ed., *The Arden Shakespeare "Hamlet,"* second series (London: Methuen, 1982).

John Dover Wilson, ed., *Hamlet,* New Shakespeare, 2nd edition (Cambridge: Cambridge University Press, 1936, rev. 1954).

My comments or alterations are inserted within brackets. Images have been resized. The name, "Shakespeare," refers to the author(s) of the works attributed to that name. Interesting arguments have been made that the works may have been written by someone other than, or in collaboration with, William Shakespeare (1564-1616). The terms "science" and "scientific" were not used in Shakespeare's time, but the methods were. Those terms are used here to mean natural or observable, repeatable, predictable means to explain phenomena.

Quotes contained in titles or headings are as follows:
"A truant disposition," spoken by Horatio (I.ii. 168).
"Th' yet unknowing world," spoken by Horatio (V.ii. 363).
"Inventors' heads," spoken by Horatio (V.ii. 369).
"The very age and body of the time," spoken by Hamlet (III.ii. 23-24).
"Aierie Images," R. Scot, *The Discoverie of Witchcraft,* bk. 13, chap. 19.
"Foul deeds will rise," spoken by Hamlet (I.ii. 255).
"True avouch of mine own eyes," spoken by Horatio (I.i. 56-57).
"The play's the thing," spoken by Hamlet (II.ii. 539).

CHAPTER ONE:

TH' YET UNKNOWING WORLD

L et us question the role of Horatio in Shakespeare's
Hamlet. More exactly, let us question the role
accepted for Horatio since the theatres reopened after
the 1660's restoration of the monarchy — six decades
after the play was written. Kenneth Branagh's (1996)
film, *HAMLET*, enlightens this questioning because
this *Hamlet* includes the characters and plotlines
Shakespeare draws to the legend. He uses the (1623)
First Folio text and from the Second Quarto (1604-
05), supplies passages missing from the First Folio.
This makes for a long play, but it helps us look past
restoration revisions back to the play Shakespeare
intended generations earlier. When Shakespeare's
characters and plotlines are fully included, it gives
the spectator opportunities to understand who the
characters are, and how their interactions — sometimes
poignant, sometimes deceptive, sometimes poignantly
deceptive — create tragic outcomes.

Despite William Shakespeare's acclaim as a great
playwright, critics suggest that *The Tragedy of Hamlet,
Prince of Denmark*, is poorly constructed and that some
of Shakespeare's unique contributions to the Hamlet
saga — the episodes with the embassy to Norway,
Polonius's instructions to Reynaldo, and Fortinbras's
mission through Denmark — are superfluous and "have

not the slightest influence on the action of the tragedy."[7] Eleanor Prosser describes the play as "shot through with inconsistencies that cannot be explained by the logic of the plot."[8] T. S. Eliot expresses even sharper criticism in his essay, "Hamlet and His Problems." Challenging inconsistencies that arise in *Hamlet*, Eliot writes, "We must simply admit that here Shakespeare tackled a problem which proved too much for him. Why he attempted it at all is an insoluble puzzle."[9] W. W. Greg urges, "We have to choose between giving up Shakespeare as a rational playwright, and giving up our inherited beliefs regarding the story of *Hamlet*."[10] No need to give up on Shakespeare as a rational playwright, but we do need to examine inherited beliefs about the play.

Many problems still have not been satisfactorily resolved. Why is Fortinbras in the play, and why does Horatio spend most of his lines talking about him? How would Shakespeare have staged the ghost's actions, appearances, and vanishing to match how these are described in spoken lines? If the ghost is Hamlet's father, why does Hamlet not recognize him? What accounts for Hamlet's bizarre, if not slapstick, behavior when he rejoins Horatio and the guards after speaking with the ghost? Why do Horatio, the guards, and Hamlet see the ghost, but Gertrude does not? How does the queen

---

[7] Roderich Benedix, "Die Shakespearomanie" (1873), in *A New Variorum Edition of Shakespeare: Hamlet*, Horace Howard Furness, ed. (Philadelphia: J. P. Lippincott, 1877), 351.

[8] Eleanor Prosser, *Hamlet and Revenge* (Stanford: Stanford University Press, 1967), 206.

[9] T. S. Eliot, "Hamlet and his Problems," *The Sacred Wood, Essays on Poetry and Criticism* (London: Methuen, 1950), 142-143.

[10] W. W. Greg, "Hamlet's Hallucination," *The Modern Language Review* 12, no. 4 (Oct 1917): 400.

know details of how Ophelia drowned, and how could someone know these close-up details but not save her? Nearly a century ago, John Dover Wilson posed similar questions in *What Happens in "Hamlet."*[11] Our questions still have not been adequately answered, despite Ian Johnston's acknowledgment that "with the exception of certain Biblical texts, no other work has produced such a continuing, lively, and contentious debate about how we are supposed to understand it."[12]

I invite the reader to reconsider persistent puzzles in *Hamlet.* From the abundance of books and commentaries published about *Hamlet,* the most convincing start with the Elizabethan-Jacobean playwright's historical circumstances and ground the action of the drama in the spoken lines of the earliest texts. Presented here is a fresh look at the roles of Horatio, the ghost, and Fortinbras. This view relies on the earliest texts and puts on the changing and often ugly mantle of the times.[13] *The Tragedy of Hamlet, Prince of Denmark,* moves Elizabethans away from medieval concepts of weaponry and courtly honor while confessing to the treacheries of powerful and murderous contemporaries. It allows spectators to see what was sometimes too risky to be written or spoken. The play shows early modern England's abuses of power and techniques of deception, weapons still vigorously

---

[11]   John Dover Wilson, *What Happens in "Hamlet,"* 3rd ed. (New York: Cambridge University Press, 1951). See Wilson's questions on pages 53-55.

[12]   Ian Johnston, "Introductory Lecture on Shakespeare's *Hamlet,*" pt. A, Feb 2001, Accessed May 2, 2008, www.mala.bc.ca/~Johnstoi/eng366/lectures/hamlet.htm.

[13]   "[T]hough Shakespeare may be for all time, he was very much of an age, and unless we grasp at least the main features of that age we are likely to miss much that is significant about him." John Dover Wilson, *The Essential Shakespeare,* (Cambridge: Cambridge University Press, 1932), 14.

used today. In *Invisible Power*, Alan Haynes describes the work of Elizabethan spymasters who sought to gather information on enemies at home and abroad. Despite difficulties with sources, Haynes asserts that "the long neglect of such a striking topic is still astonishing" and that "rarefied ideas of historical scholarship and polite truth do not sit easily with mendacity, betrayal, apostacy, double dealing, false witness, torture and executions."[14]

The long neglect of Horatio's intended role is also astonishing. Although more has been written about *Hamlet* than any other piece of English literature, David Ball writes that "somehow in all that scrutiny the obvious has been lost, so you must find it yourself."[15] The obvious is that Shakespeare intended a crucial, textured, and to some degree, villainous role for Horatio. Staging Horatio in cooperation with Fortinbras to bring down King Claudius resolves some apparent inconsistencies. Since the mid-1660s, Horatio has been identified as Hamlet's friend, even in the playbill's List of Roles (*Dramatis Personae*). However, the List of Roles, in which Horatio is identified as "Hamlet's friend and fellow student," did not appear in a printing of Shakespeare's *Hamlet* until 1667 — fifty years after William Shakespeare had died. The List of Roles is not in any of the three earlier printed texts (the 1603 First Quarto, Q1; the 1604 Second Quarto, Q2; and the 1623 First Folio, F1), but it appears in editions subsequent to 1667. So now, before the curtain even opens, these alterations compromise the playwright's creation, the

---

14   Alan Haynes, *Invisible Power: The Elizabethan Secret Services, 1570-1603* (New York: St. Martin's Press, 1992), vii.

15   David Ball, *Backwards and Forwards: A Technical Manual for Reading Plays* (Carbondale, IL: Southern Illinois University Press, 1983), 47.

director's stage, and playgoers' assumptions of the play. Such revisions/alterations would be skewed by decades of political upheaval and official censorship. The registry of performance for Shakespeare's *Hamlet* during his lifetime (he died in 1616) is mostly empty, with the (disputed) exception of a 1607 off-shore performance aboard a ship.[16] There were fires; the Globe theater burned down in 1613. Outbreaks of plague often closed the theaters. There was civil war; the king was beheaded (1649), and theaters were forced to close for two decades until the restoration of the monarchy. This history complicates the fact that we do not know how the play was actually performed in Shakespeare's time and allows us to speculate that the play was probably censored.

The editors of the 2007 Arden Shakespeare edition, Taylor and Thompson, also question Horatio's role.[17] An apparent citizen of Elsinore, Horatio has knowledge of Danish politics and is on friendly terms with the guards. But Hamlet refers to Horatio as a visitor to Elsinore, and the guards refer to him as a scholar. What is to be made of his "long periods of silence onstage"? (p. 143). The editors find it odd that in Act 1, scene 2, Horatio "seems to be on a brief and unsanctioned (*truant* in line 168) visit from the university" (p. 180). And, in the last scene of the play, "Horatio, enigmatic throughout, becomes even more baffling" (p. 136). He promises to tell "th' yet unknowing world how things came about" then speaks generally of murders or plots.

---

[16]   Thompson and Taylor, eds., *Arden Shakespeare "Hamlet,"* 53-57; also
        see Janette Dillon, *The Cambridge Introduction to Early English Theatre.*
        (Cambridge: Cambridge University Press, 2006), 218-220.

[17]   Thompson and Taylor, *Arden Shakespeare "Hamlet."*

He does not tell the onstage audience any "specific details (about the death of old Hamlet, or the King's plots against young Hamlet, for example) that are known to the theatre audience or reader" (p. 462).[18]

Horatio's role is intended to be somewhere between misguided and sinister, giving directors wide latitude. Even if Horatio is identified as Prince Hamlet's friend, as Hamlet himself greets him in the first act, it does not mean he truly acts as a friend. This dichotomy weaves a more tragic and textured relationship. Shakespeare effectively uses the concept of betrayed or misguided trust in several plays. Examples include the perhaps unintended betrayal by Iago's wife in *Othello*; the well-intended but tragic intervention of the Friar in *Romeo and Juliet*; and Lord Scroop's betrayal of Henry V, in *Henry V*. A more severe example is seen in the wickedly calculated betrayal of Othello by Iago, who, like Horatio, plays the friend and loyal servant. Lacey Baldwin Smith describes an enemy disguised as a friend: "[I]n a sense, [*Othello*] belongs to the advice-book genre: a dreadful admonition against innocent trust of a friend who is in fact the enemy in disguise ... It is blind trust ... that makes possible Iago's treachery. Almost to the very end, when the audience is itching to cry out and warn the noble Moor not to be so gullible, Iago remains 'my friend ... honest, honest Iago.'"[19]

Although Shakespeare's text makes it clear to spectators that Iago should not have been trusted, the trust factor with Horatio is not so clear. While Horatio and Hamlet's friendship is questionable, their fellowship as students at Wittenberg is not. Horatio

---

18   Thompson and Taylor, *Arden Shakespeare "Hamlet."*

19   Lacey Baldwin Smith, *Treason in Tudor England: Politics and Paranoia* (Princeton, NJ: Princeton University Press, 1986), 70.

would have known young Hamlet and would have
known that he suffered from what was then called
"melancholia." At Wittenberg, Hamlet would have
been recognized as the most likely heir to the throne of
Denmark. Within months, Hamlet and Horatio learn
that old King Hamlet has died and that Hamlet, the son,
has been passed over in the election to king. Claudius,
old Hamlet's brother, takes the throne and marries
Hamlet's mother, Gertrude–a marriage Hamlet
believes is wrong. These events, added to perceived
and real betrayals, intensify his nerve disease, or
melancholia. He lapses into and out of brilliance and
foolishness, intensity and despair. Horatio, knowing
Hamlet is losing concentration and emotional stability,
also knows that this affliction would make Hamlet a
weak, vulnerable, and incompetent ruler for Denmark.
Politically astute Horatio joins forces with Fortinbras to
overthrow Claudius–thus securing power for himself
and possibly, a token kingship for Hamlet.

Martin Scofield writes that C. S. Lewis saw *Hamlet*
essentially as the story of "a man who has been given a
task by a ghost." Scofield would amend that to say that the
play is essentially "the story of a man who has been given
a task by his father's ghost."[20] I would amend that further
to say that *Hamlet* is essentially the story of a man who
is given a criminal task by someone pretending to be his
father's ghost. The ghost is a cowardly attempt to coerce
Hamlet into killing Claudius. Again, the List of Roles,
identifying the ghost as "the Ghost of Hamlet's father,"
is a late seventeenth-century invention. Wilson reminds
us that a proper understanding of the ghost is important
and "no mere side-issue or antiquarian interest: what is

---

[20] Martin Scofield, *The Ghosts of Hamlet: The Play and Modern Writers*
(Cambridge: Cambridge University Press, 1980), 113, 138.

7

involved is nothing less than Shakespeare's reputation as a dramatist."[21] Horatio brings Hamlet to the ghost to set the tragedy in motion. Directors, playgoers, and Hamlet wonder if the ghost is from hell. The ghost comes from foreign and castle-insider intrigue — likely a metaphorical, but not a supernatural, hell. Shakespeare nudges contemporaries away from sixteenth-century superstition and into modern Europe by presenting the ghost as a hoax. While Horatio pretends the apparition is a ghost, Hamlet suspects the ghost is knavery. Hamlet, the modern scholar, takes instruction from Scot: "[W]heresoever you shall heare, that there is in the night season such rumbling and fearefull noises [the ghost], be you well assured that it is flat knaverie, performed by some that is ... least mistrusted [Horatio]."[22] In Act 1, scene 5, Hamlet recognizes the magician's trick, "Hic et ubique," meaning here and everywhere.

Horatio has become one of Fortinbras's "lawless resolutes," working on the inside to bring down Claudius. The recent death of old Hamlet benefited young Fortinbras because it reopened his claim on

[21] Wilson, *What Happens in "Hamlet,"* 55.

[22] The following quote provides an example for how the scholar Hamlet would understand that the ghost is a trick, even if well-played. "Cardanus speaking of noises, among other things, saith thus: A noise is heard in your house; it may be a mouse, a cat, or a dog among dishes; it may be counterfet or a theefe indeed, or the fault may be in your eares. ... [Men] have even forsaken their houses, bicause of such apparitions and noises: and all hath beene by meere and ranke knaverie. And wheresoever you shall heare, that there is in the night season such rumbling and fearefull noises, be you well assured that it is flat knaverie, performed by some that is ... least mistrusted. ... The divell seeketh dailie as well as nightlie whome he may devoure ..." Reginald Scot, *The Discoverie of Witchcraft* (London: William Brome, 1584; republished with an introduction by Montague Summers, London: J. Rodker, 1930), bk. 15, chap. 40.

lands lost to Denmark. This loss resulted from a wager between two now-dead kings. Fortinbras believes old Hamlet's death nullifies the defeat of his father, old Fortinbras, by Hamlet's father, old Hamlet. With Claudius out of the way, Fortinbras could regain his father's rights to lands in the kingdom. In return, young Fortinbras would offer a ruling position (Principal Secretary) to Horatio and security for the royal Dane, Prince Hamlet. This plan misfires and piles up more dead bodies than we would suppose the conspirators desired.[23] It goes awry when Hamlet is too modern to accept an order to murder from a ghost. He is too moral to kill someone without reflection, corroboration, and proof of guilt. He is too unnerved and unstable to be calculating even in small things, let alone murder. He is also too "free of all contriving" to easily accept the readiness of others to contrive against him.[24]

Reputed to be a scholar, Horatio's words reveal one who has knowledge of the history, wars, and politics of Denmark, Norway, and ancient Rome. He speaks from an intelligence perspective, and Shakespeare would not give him a positive role. He has befriended the castle guards. Addressed as "sir," he is powerful enough to give people access to the king. He is apparently trusted by King Claudius and Queen Gertrude. When Hamlet is sent off to England, Horatio remains in attendance to them. When Ophelia comes before them, apparently mad, Claudius asks Horatio to look after her: "Follow her close; give her good watch, I pray you" (IV.v.). This occurs just before

---

[23]   "Of accidental judgments, casual slaughters ... And in the upshot, purposes mistook fallen on the inventors' heads," Act 5, scene 2.

[24]   See Claudius's opinion of his nephew, Hamlet, in Act 4, scene 7: "[Hamlet], being remiss, most generous, and free from all contriving, will not peruse the foils ..."

Ophelia is reported drowned. In the next to last scene, they will also ask Horatio to keep watch on Hamlet: "I pray thee good Horatio, wait upon him" (V.i.).

In contrast to Horatio's sometimes verbose and often influential stage presence, we hear little from Fortinbras. In Calderwood's *To Be or Not to Be*, Fortinbras is described as "moving silently at the edges of the play, raising armies against Denmark, employing them against Poland, appearing suddenly amid the carnage of the final scene to receive Hamlet's dying vote, taking charge of Hamlet's funeral, and preparing to assert his title to the Danish throne."[25] Fortinbras stages a march on Poland through Denmark to be in position to storm Elsinore. Fortinbras's army in Denmark is the "late innovation," the political disturbance that has taken the players out of the city and put them on the road as a traveling company.[26] When word reaches Fortinbras of the duel between Hamlet and Laertes, he rushes with warlike noise to storm Elsinore. What Fortinbras finds is mass slaughter. His army only has to occupy the castle and help with the burials. The plot to get Hamlet

---

[25] James L. Calderwood, *To Be or Not to Be: Negation and Metadrama in "Hamlet"* (New York: Columbia University Press, 1983), 12.

[26] The word *innovation*, "usually connoted a challenge to the established order and often had the specific sense of an uprising." It has this sense in other Shakespearean writings. "Unless Fortinbras's 'enterprise' should be thought to qualify" as the innovation, "it is not easily traceable in the plot of the play." As Jenkins sees it, Shakespeare is referring to a political disturbance, "and if the passage is rightly dated after February 1601, [he] must have done so in the knowledge, if not with the design, that the audience would instantly identify 'the late innovation' with the Essex rebellion." Harold Jenkins, ed., *The Arden Shakespeare "Hamlet,"* 2nd ser. (London: Methuen, 1982), 471-472. And see also Thompson and Taylor, *Arden Shakespeare "Hamlet,"* 259, "Editors have interpreted the late innovation as a reference to political disturbances — perhaps the death of the elder Hamlet and the preparations for war in the Danish context, or the Essex rebellion in 1601 if an English topical allusion is intended."

to kill Claudius overreaches, taking seven additional people to their graves. Horatio presents Hamlet with a trick ghost to urge him to murder Claudius. What most remember first about the fall of Troy is the trick of the Trojan horse, not the son seeking revenge. But for revenge loyalists, *Hamlet* can still be viewed as a revenge play. The initial revenge seekers are Fortinbras and Horatio (followed by Hamlet and Laertes). Fortinbras wants to nullify his father's defeat and regain lost territory; he wants the rights to his father's kingdom restored. Horatio wants to revenge young Hamlet's, and indirectly his own, recent slights and losses, thus gaining power for himself.

Others have recognized Horatio and Fortinbras as at least co-beneficiaries, if not co-conspirators. This study offers examples. Michael Innes (J. I. M. Stewart) identified Horatio and Fortinbras as co-conspirators against Claudius. In "The Mysterious Affair at Elsinore," Innes sees Shakespeare's play as an unsolved murder mystery, with Fortinbras himself as the architect of the "vantage he so promptly turned up to claim."[27] Innes asks that we examine the train of events and then ask who benefited. He writes, "Had Horatio already been squared, and was Fortinbras secure in the knowledge that his future Lord Chamberlain [Horatio] ... would have nothing material to say 'to the yet unknowing world'?"[28]

Alethea Hayter's novel, *Horatio's Version*, gives Horatio the opportunity to tell Hamlet's story. Horatio shares notes from his own journal before the court

27   Rayner Heppenstall and Michael Innes, *Three Tales of Hamlet* (London: Gollancz, 1950), 75-89.

28   Heppenstall and Innes, *Three Tales of Hamlet*, 87. (Similarly, after the death of Queen Elizabeth, Robert Cecil assures the accession of James to the throne of England and becomes his Lord Secretary.)

11

of enquiry appointed by the new king, Fortinbras.[29] Fortinbras wants the facts behind the deaths to be made clear to the public. Voltemand presides over this enquiry where interesting observations and speculations arise from the testimonies of survivors. Lee Blessing's comedy, *Fortinbras,* starts where the bodies are being carried off at the end of *Hamlet.*[30] Fortinbras appoints Horatio to structure Hamlet's story to improve Fortinbras's public image.

My interpretation is neither a prequel nor a sequel. It does not eliminate characters or story lines. It is derived from the spoken lines of the early texts (Q1, Q2, and F1) and requires that Horatio's character be played as university associate of Hamlet and conspirator against Claudius. It may be difficult to give up centuries of seeing Horatio as Hamlet's two-dimensional sidekick. But Shakespeare often challenges characters with conflicting loyalties, unintended outcomes, and pretended, mistaken, or hidden identities. Horatio's identity as a partner with Fortinbras against Claudius (but not necessarily against Hamlet) makes his character more interesting and believable. It also makes his relationship with Hamlet more deeply tragic.

Oscar Wilde asks, "Are the critics of *Hamlet* mad, or are they just pretending to be?"[31] One could also ask if we have forgotten that *Hamlet* is a play and not a sacred text. Enjoyable interpretations would not leave unwrapped the playwright's extraordinary gift for subtle depths of character, layers of intrigue, and tragically misguided

---

[29]   Alethea Hayter, *Horatio's Version* (London: Faber and Faber, 1972).

[30]   Lee Blessing, "Fortinbras," *Patient A and Other Plays* (Portsmouth, NH: Heinemann Drama, 1995).

[31]   Attributed to Oscar Wilde in Martin Scofield's *The Ghosts of Hamlet,* page 60.

purposes. Although the words, words, words in *Hamlet* form such rich literature that the play succeeds anyway, it is more than high quality prose with royalty, clowns, murders, and a ghost. Encouraged here are staged interpretations that more adequately imagine stage directions and character developments embedded in the spoken lines of the early texts — interpretations that "suit the action to the word, the word to the action" (III.ii 17). My interpretation unites themes, plots, and story lines. It resolves some nagging inconsistencies about the play, makes characters more believable, and more satisfactorily reveals the play's political context. The following chapters support this interpretation and guide the reader through some of the whys and hows. We will rely upon the three earliest texts, visit pertinent religious and political events in Shakespeare's England, and reimagine Shakespeare's novel use of the ghost. The final chapter suggests some staging ideas for this view of *Hamlet*.

INVENTORS' HEADS

Horatio and Fortinbras plan to eliminate Claudius by coercing a resentful, unstable, and passed-over king (Prince Hamlet) to kill the king. From inside Elsinore, Horatio collaborates with Francisco, Voltemand, and Osric. As a palace guard, Francisco may have witnessed King Hamlet's murder, so it may be from Francisco that their spokesman, the ghost, knows Claudius murdered old Hamlet. (Claudius admits in prayer to the murder [III.iii.], but he does not admit to the details we hear from the ghost or see in the Gonzago play.) The guards would also be in a period of adjustment to or denial of Claudius as king. It would be natural for them to harbor loyalties to old Hamlet and disappointment that young Hamlet is not king.

Voltemand, an ambassador, is a double agent, a turncoat, as his name implies. Voltemand's name is sometimes printed as "Valtemand" (Q2), "Voltumand" (F1), and "Voltemar" (Q1). "Volte," from the French *volti*, the Italian *volta*, and the Latin *volo*, means a turn, a shift, or change. *Volte-face*, for example, means an "about-face, a reversal of judgment, belief, or policy."[32] "Mand" can be understood as the order or commission from the Latin *mandare* — to order, commission, or hand-deliver, from the Latin *manus* meaning hand. Another possibility is that "mand" is Danish for man. The Danish *mand* can also mean troops (men) or an adherent. Although Voltemand's name has been described as "a corruption of 'Valdemar,' the name of several Danish kings," his name implies one who reverses an order, a turncoat, or double agent.[33]

Osric, a wealthy land steward, provides for the king's table. Osric's lands include those old Fortinbras forfeited to King Hamlet. Maintaining his lands and livelihood would depend on the favor of the king, and Osric would seek favor from whoever is king. Like Hamlet and Fortinbras, Osric is sometimes referred to as "young" Osric. Like Hamlet, Fortinbras and (later) Laertes, Osric is motivated by a father's loss. While the last scene of the play might make it "very easy to laugh at Osric, Shakespeare shows that it is also easy to underestimate him."[34]

[32] World Book Dictionary (Chicago: Doubleday, 1977), s. v. "volte-face."

[33] Harold Jenkins, editor of *The Arden Shakespeare "Hamlet"* (1982), references the name as a corruption of the name for several Danish kings on page 163.

[34] Jan H. Blits, *Deadly Thought: Hamlet and the Human Soul* (Lanham, MD: Lexington Books, 2001), 361.

Horatio presents Marcellus, Barnardo, and Hamlet with a ghost to communicate the plea for revenge to Hamlet. Sixteenth-century author Reginald Scot describes how Horatio tries to influence Hamlet.

Publike confederacie is, when there is before hand a compact made betwixt diverse persons; the one to be principall, the rest to be as assistants in working of miracles, or rather in cousening and abusing the beholders. As when I tell you in the presence of [others] what you have thought or doone, or shall doo or thinke, when you and I were thereupon agreed before. And if this be cunninglie and closelie handled, it will induce great admiration to the beholders; speciallie when they are before amazed and abused by some experiments of naturall magike ...[35]

The play tells us that Horatio has been at Wittenberg University with Hamlet, is recognized as a scholar, and "we feel we know Hamlet's friend so well that it never occurs to us to ask questions about him."[36] Horatio first identifies himself as one among "friends to this ground," while Marcellus adds both as among "liegemen to the Dane." When the guards ask him if he is Horatio, he responds that he is "a piece of him." He uses informal and soldierly conversational terms with the guards and refers to old Hamlet as "our" last king, and Denmark as "our state." He is well informed about Danish history and politics. Hamlet calls him "friend" but responds to him as if he's not sure he is Horatio: "Horatio, or do I forget myself?" Horatio offers him no condolences for the loss of his father, the "goodly king," whom Horatio claims to have known.

---

[35]   Scot, *Discoverie of Witchcraft*, bk. 13, chap. 14.

[36]   John Dover Wilson, ed., *Hamlet*, New Shakespeare, 2nd ed. (Cambridge: Cambridge University Press, 1936, rev. 1954), xlix.

When he speaks to Hamlet, Hamlet remarks that he speaks falsely. ("Nor shall you do my ear that violence to make it truster of your own report against thyself, I know you are no truant" [I.ii.].) Does Horatio's admitted "truant disposition" mean he is not authorized to be at Elsinore? Christopher Warley describes another sense of "truant" from the Old English as, "one who begs without justification; a sturdy beggar ... an idle rogue or knave."[37] Warley then offers that Hamlet has the more truant disposition by idly "playing hooky from his obligation to kill Claudius."[38] I would argue that Horatio is the truant, by making a show of the poor and humble servant while being a clever and controlling knave.

A key to the tragedy is there, in lines from the first scene of the play:

Who's there?
[Again] Who is there?
Is Horatio there?

Although Q1 places Rosencrantz and Guildenstern at Wittenberg with Horatio, there are curiously no spoken lines and no apparent camaraderie among the three. And unlike Laertes, Ophelia, and Hamlet, the play does not tell us who Horatio's parents are. At least "a piece of" Horatio is a stranger to Denmark—he doesn't know who Yorick was (V.i.) and says he is ignorant of court customs (I.iv.). When Horatio comments (I.iv.), "[B]ut this is wondrous strange," Hamlet counters by telling him he should welcome strange since Horatio himself is a stranger. It seems Hamlet is saying Horatio was born outside of Denmark. Did Horatio first come

---

37   Christopher Warley, "Specters of Horatio," *ELH* 75, no. 4 (Winter 2008): 1031.

38   Warley, "Specters of Horatio," 1031.

to Denmark as a foreign mercenary? Did Horatio serve old Hamlet as a spy? Was he employed by old Hamlet's court as one of Polonius's spies to monitor Hamlet at Wittenberg? In either role, as mercenary or spy, Horatio would represent a certain danger; his loyalty could belong to the highest bidder. The name "Horatio" could refer to ancient Rome's Horace, who, though a wartime traitor to the eventual victor, was welcomed back to and flourished within the government he had betrayed.[39] Horace was not born to a noble family and had to find other means to succeed. His father sacrificed to send the young Horace to university. While there, he established friendships with noble young Romans.[40] After the assassination of Julius Caesar, a civil war broke out in Rome, and Horace joined Brutus's forces against Julius's successors. Upon hearing that a fellow rebel had been killed in battle, Brutus killed himself. Horace, however, fled the battle and made his way back to Rome, where he slowly ingratiated himself with his former adversaries in government, including Caesar Augustus. He acquired a comfortable position as a civil servant and became respected as orator, poet, and historian. At play's end, after Horatio describes himself as more the "antique Roman," it is the task of truthful historian that Hamlet asks Horatio to undertake.[41]

---

[39] Horace, whose full name was Quintus Horatius Flaccus, lived 65 B.C.-8 B.C.

[40] Peter Levi provides biographical information in *Horace: A Life* (London: Duckworth, 1997).

[41] In "*Hamlet's* Horatio as an Allusion to Horace's *Odes*," Jacob Sider Jost reviews possible sources for the name "Horatio," then proposes that the name "is intended to recall the Roman poet, Horace." When Barnardo asks if Horatio is there, Horatio answers, "a piece of him" (I.i. 18). Sider Jost notes that "a piece of him" is a quote from one of Horaces's odes. He argues that Horatio, like Horace, "becomes a medium of posthumous literary survival." See Jacob Sider Jost, "*Hamlet's* Horatio

17

Horatio presents another correlation between Horace and himself just before the ghost's second appearance in Act 1, scene 1. He goes to oratorical lengths to ease the guards' acceptance of the apparition as the ghost of the old king, even offering that ghosts were coming out of their graves a little before Julius Caesar fell, too. This portended disaster for Caesar.

The ghost appears in full battle armor. That armor conveniently, maybe humorously, obscures gait, mannerisms, and facial features. In each of the three early texts, Horatio tells the guards that the ghost's armor was like the very armor the king wore "when he the ambitious Norway combated" (I.i.). Later, in answering Hamlet's questions about the ghost, all three texts have Horatio state that the ghost appeared in full battle armor, from head to foot (capapea/cap-a-pie).[42] Battle armor precludes parade or ceremonial armor and helps set time limits for the kings' duel. By the mid-sixteenth century, full armor, though still produced for show (tournament, parade, and ceremony), had become too cumbersome for use in battle. Gunpowder and the use of firearms made full battle armor more of a trap than a protection. As firearms increased in power and number, armor needed to increase in weight, thus decreasing the wearer's mobility and making full armor too heavy; some weighed more than 50 pounds. Full battlefield armor means the kings' duel happened before 1540. To set the duel's earlier time limit, Wittenberg University (in each of the early texts),

as an Allusion to Horace's *Odes*," *Notes and Queries* 59, no. 1 (March 2012): 76-77.

[42] "Such was the armour he had on when he the ambitious Norway combated. So frowned he once, when ... [he] smote the sledded Polacks ..." (I.i. 59-62) and "Armed at point, exactly, cap-a-pie, ..." (I.ii. 199).

where Horatio and Hamlet (and in Q1, Rosencrantz and Guildenstern) have been students, was founded in 1502. The duel and Hamlet's birth were the same day (V.i. 135-140), and since Hamlet would be at least twelve or so to attend university, the earliest date for the duel would be within a decade of 1480 — widely setting the time limits for the kings' duel between about 1475 and 1540.

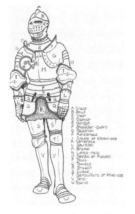 

Figure 1. Ffoukles[43]   Figure 2. Demmin[44]

[43]   Charles Ffoukles, *Armour and Weapons* (Oxford: Clarendon Press, 1909), 73.

[44]   August Demmin, *Die Kriegswaffen — Ein Handbuch der Waffenkunde* (Leipzig: Seemann, 1869), Kaiserliches Arsenal-Wien, Imperial Armoury-Vienna, 218.

Details of armor would matter to Shakespeare's generation who had seen full battle armor disappear from the battlefield. As Bert Hall instructs, "The tension between seeing the sixteenth century as the last medieval age and seeing it as the seedbed of the modern world is inescapable in respect to the specific problems of how to interpret military and political changes in this period."[45] Armor details from the relevant time span (1475-1540) are necessary to fulfill Shakespeare's dramatic intent. In figure 1, we see cap-a-pie armor from the relevant time span.

The armor in figure 2 is from the early 1500s with a visor/bevor that can be lifted. At the close of the fifteenth century, Italian and German styles of armor merged, and armor from this time has similar appearance in England and northern Europe.[46] This style, usually more embellished than battlefield armor, has become known as the Maximilian style after the Emperor Maximilian, who reigned 1493-1519.

---

[45]   Bert S. Hall, *Weapons and Warfare in Renaissance Europe* (Baltimore: Johns Hopkins University Press, 1997), 201.

[46]   R. Ewart Oakeshott, *A Knight and His Armour* (London: Camelot Press, 1961), 50.

Figure 3.   Figure 4.

Fig. 3. (ABOVE LEFT) Armor of the reign of Henry VII, 1485-1509 ("in the Meyrick collection"), James Robinson Planché, *History of British Costume,* New Edition (London: C. Cox & printed by Clowes and Sons, 1847), page 281. Courtesy of Special Collections, Kenneth Spencer Research Library, University of Kansas Libraries. Fig. 4. (ABOVE RIGHT) "Suit of armour for fighting on foot, King Henry VIII (Tower of London)," Charles Henry Ashdown, *British and Foreign Arms and Armour* (London: T. C. and E. C. Jack, 1909), 287.

Figure 3 is from the reign of England's King Henry VII (1485-1509), who won his crown when his forces defeated those of Richard III on the battlefield. The figure provides an example of armor toward our earlier time limit (1475). The helmet opened by throwing up the lower part that guarded the chin and throat, together with the visor, which turned upon the same screw.[47] Also, see the complete armor (ca. 1497) of Germany's Schott von Hellingen on page 83 in Oakeshott's *A Knight and His Armour.*[48]

---

[47]   James Robinson Planché, *History of British Costume,* new ed. (London: C. Cox, 1847), 282.

[48]   Oakeshott, *A Knight and His Armour.*

The ghost-king's armor could resemble the complete armor for Henry VIII (Figure 4), which weighs nearly 100 pounds. This would represent armor toward the later time limit. In addition to cap-a-pie battle armor, all three texts state that the king wears his beaver up.[49] The beaver is generally understood as the part that protects the mouth and chin area. In some earlier armor, the beaver is stationary. Later, it could be pulled down from the helmet to reveal the mouth, while the visor, protecting the eyes, could be pulled up. By the fifteenth century, the visor and the part of the beaver covering the mouth area sometimes combine to form one piece. This could attach to the helmet at the side and pivot upwards to reveal the eyes and the mouth.

Horatio tells the guards that the ghost looked frowningly and later tells Hamlet that it looked more sorrowful than angry. Facial details, in the night shadow of the raised beaver, would not have been distinct on a bearded figure (I.ii. 237-239). It puzzles Hamlet, Marcellus, and Barnardo that Horatio would claim to know details of the bearded ghost's facial expression. A cited reference for Horatio's claim that he could see the ghost's face because "he wore his beaver up" (I.ii. 228) is the *Cyclopedia of Costume,* Volume 1, published in 1876.[50] The *Cyclopedia's* entry for "beaver" references Shakespeare's *Hamlet* but illustrates early

---

[49]   The beaver is also referred to as the bevor, beavor, baviere, Kinnstueck, mentonniere. "Many are the derivations suggested for this word. ... Shakespeare's use of the word rather suggests that he is alluding to a moveable attachment to the helmet." Shakespeare also uses the word in *Henry IV, Pt. 2,* Act 4, scene 1, and in *Richard III,* Act 5, scene 3. And see Guy Francis Laking's, *Catalogue of the European Armour and Arms in the Wallace Collection at Hertford House* (London: His Majesty's Stationery Office, 1901), 45-46.

[50]   James Robinson Planché, *Cyclopedia of Costume,* vol. 1 (London: Clowes, 1876), 38-39.

fifteenth-century armor, dating several decades before 1475. Planché furnishes a more helpful illustration for *Hamlet* on page 285 of the same *Cyclopedia of Costume*, Volume 1. Here we see helmets from the relevant time span with beavers/visors that could be worn up.[51]

Hamlet would also puzzle over his fellow scholar's enthusiastic acceptance that what has appeared to him and the guards is a ghost. Wittenberg, the place of learning Shakespeare adds (in each early text) to the Hamlet legend, is where the Catholic monk Martin Luther nailed his ninety-five theses to the castle church door (1517). These challenges led to the Protestant Reformation. At Wittenberg, Horatio and Hamlet would probably have learned the Protestant teaching that ghosts no longer appear, except as harmful apparitions or cozenage. Well-meaning spirits may exist, but they do not have to take on form (appear). Hamlet is patiently perplexed that Horatio would make these claims about battle armor and a ghost.

Horatio withholds or provides information to control others. This relates him to the Elizabethan-Jacobean secret service and to Shakespeare's powerful political contemporaries, such as Robert Cecil — spymaster, information chief, and the country's leading politician. Like Horatio, R. Cecil was skilled with words and well-positioned to control stories. Later in this book, R. Cecil is identified as a force behind the execution of Essex and as the link between James VI and the English throne. Shakespeare reveals his contemporary, also known as "Robert the Devil," through Horatio as deceiver, benefactor and surviving storyteller.

Shakespeare's creation, Fortinbras (in each of the early texts), is a threatening, ambitious, and readily

---

51   Planché, *Cyclopedia of Costume*, 285.

deceiving young prince. At the death of old Hamlet, he becomes an unpredictable threat to Denmark's diminished kingdom. With Hamlet's last breaths, he begs Horatio to truthfully tell Hamlet's story. When that "water-fly," Osric, makes his report, the dying Hamlet learns it is Fortinbras who has been making warlike noise to enter the castle unannounced. Hamlet acknowledges the coup and the "confederacie" that will envelop the truth. Fortinbras and Horatio meet on center stage. Fortinbras addresses Horatio as if he were responding to a message, "Where is this sight?"

TEXT MESSAGES

We do not know what Shakespeare's master copy of *Hamlet* looked like. We do not know how the play was performed in Shakespeare's time. Two revised versions, the "most valuable scripts for understanding how *Hamlet* was actually performed, no longer exist."[52] Shakespeare's theatrical contribution to the Hamlet/ Amleth saga demands a skillful, insightful director.

An early source of the story, written by a Dane, Saxo Grammaticus, in his *History of the Danes,* may date from as early as the second half of the twelfth century. Shakespeare would have been familiar with several narratives with a main character of Hamlet, or Amleth. The playwright may have borrowed from Belleforest's *Histoires Tragique* (Paris 1582), Kyd's *Spanish Tragedy,*[53] and *Der Bestrafte Brudermord* (Fratricide Punished). (Conversely, *Bestrafte Brudermord* may be borrowed from Shakespeare.) Because we have no copy of a so-called *Ur-Hamlet,* referenced in

---

[52]   Shapiro, *A Year in the Life of William Shakespeare,* 316.

[53]   Thomas Kyd was arrested in May 1593 and charged with "libel that concerned the state." Wilson, *Hamlet,* New Shakespeare, xix, xxi. in

secondary literature as performed in the decade or so before Shakespeare's *Hamlet,* it is impossible to know what Shakespeare may have borrowed from it.

As early as 1594, the year Shakespeare's acting company first performed at court, a version of the *Hamlet* story was performed by his company. Shakespeare later crafted his own uniquely powerful, turn of the century version of the tragedy. His version was likely first performed around 1600, but no printed copy survives from that time.

In that time, publication meant presenting the play to the public on stage, not necessarily preserving a printed edition of the play. Plays were written for performance, not printing—they were "not books, but scripts designed to be realized on stage."[54] Copyright laws as we know them did not exist, so a playwright risked losing a publicly printed form of his work to another theater company.[55] Shakespeare's company would have had only one or two master copies. Copies needed to be handwritten, and fewer copies made it less likely the script would be stolen by another company. Actors received only a copy of their individual parts, not a complete copy of the play. Surviving texts of Shakespeare's *Hamlet* may have used copies of particular actors' parts to help in reconstructing the text. Versions of *Hamlet* attributed to Shakespeare but never signed by him were printed in (or within months of) 1603, 1604, and 1623. Thomas Clayton's book, *The "Hamlet" First Published* (Q1, 1603), provides useful essays about the early texts. I found Kathleen Irace's essay particularly helpful. Her visual on page 119 ("Conjectural Relationship between Q1, Q2, and F"), neatly organizes

---

[54] Shapiro, *A Year in the Life of William Shakespeare,* 316.

[55] Russ McDonald, *The Bedford Companion to Shakespeare: An Introduction with Documents* (Boston: Bedford Books Boston, 1996), 76.

the text processes.[56] We do not know the relationship between the early texts and how they were performed.

This book views the three earliest texts through the lens of the tumultuous political period in which Shakespeare wrote the play. Today's *Hamlet*, (*Hamlets*) Shakespeare's longest play, contains incomplete, disputed, and possibly pirated best guesses. As Thompson and Taylor point out, "Nearly four hundred years later, there is still no consensus on what constitutes the true text of *Hamlet*."[57] Stephen Orgel seems to concur and asks, "What texts? ... [N]one of our texts is original ... every word we possess by Shakespeare has been through some editorial process."[58]

Along with a lack of a definitive text, comes a lack of reliable stage directions for the text. Typically, only the director (manager or playwright) would have the play's master copy, into which he could add, remove, or adjust stage directions. Shakespeare scholar W. W. Greg "maintained that the playwright would usually not provide stage directions in his manuscript but would 'leave a blank for the direction' to be later filled in after the actors had worked out the mechanics of the action in rehearsal."[59] E. A. J. Honigmann states that Shakespeare was "careless about stage-directions," and that some directions were added or misplaced by scriveners or added by eighteenth-century editors. In accepting these (and other) assumptions, Honigmann therefore asserts that "we cannot avoid giving a higher authority

[56] Kathleen Irace, "Origins and Agents of Q1 *Hamlet*," in *The "Hamlet" First Published (Q1, 1603): Origins, Form, Intertextualities*, ed. Thomas Clayton (Newark DE: University of Delaware Press, 1992), 90-122.

[57] Thompson and Taylor, *Arden Shakespeare "Hamlet,"* 486.

[58] Orgel, *The Authentic Shakespeare*, 35.

[59] Eric Rasmussen, "Afterword," in *Stage Directions in "Hamlet,"* ed. Hardin L. Aasand (Madison, NJ: Fairleigh Dickinson University Press, 2003), 226.

to the 'implied stage-directions' of the dialogue than to directions printed as such."[60] He contends that "we have a great opportunity, and a great responsibility: to see the plays, not as editors direct, but as we would wish to direct them ourselves."[61] Fortunately, editors increasingly give more authority to stage directions implied in the dialogue than to printed stage directions.[62]

Though accused of carelessness, it is likely Shakespeare was more cautious than careless with stage directions. It would have been safer for the playwright to avoid writing some stage directions into the script. As early as 1570, the theater was attacked as fostering immorality and hypocrisy.[63] How could one be a Christian if he played the part of the devil? Attackers claimed the theater taught people how to lie, deceive, swear, blaspheme, be proud, haughty, arrogant, and "become bawd, unclean, and ... devirginate maids; ... murder, ... rob, rebel against princes, commit treasons ... practice idleness ..."[64] Interestingly, Francis Walsingham, Puritan head of the spy service, defended the theater. Under state control, he could use the stage to advance the state's causes and censor or malign other causes. The government used satires, histories, and even sermons to prop up positions.

A law against conjuring would have made a playwright think twice before writing conjuring (optical

---

60   E. A. J. Honigmann, *Myriad-Minded Shakespeare: Essays, Chiefly on the Tragedies and Problem Comedies* (New York: St. Martin's Press, 1989), 187.

61   Honigmann, *Myriad-Minded Shakespeare*, 187.

62   Alan C. Dessen, *Rescripting Shakespeare: The Text, the Director, and Modern Productions* (Cambridge: Cambridge University Press, 2002), 136.

63   McDonald, *Bedford Companion to Shakespeare*, 318.

64   Philip Stubbes, "The Anatomy of Abuses" (1583), in *Bedford Companion to Shakespeare*, 341.

illusion) into the script. Techniques for projecting ghosts may have been considered conjuring. Plays showing rebellion or deposition were also barred from court. Play scripts had to pass a court censor before they could be approved for print or performance; it was safer to leave some actions imagined from context or spoken lines, rather than written down. Few copies, director autonomy, the lack of a definitive (uncensored?) text, printer errors or additions, and the fear of political or legal reprisals leave few reliable directions but greater freedom for directors to discern the play Shakespeare intended. Johnston encourages directors: "[b]ecause there is so much ambiguity and uncertainty about many key elements, *Hamlet* offers a director a great deal of creative scope, and hence the variety in productions of this play is unmatched in all Shakespeare, perhaps in all tragic drama."[65]

Remaining texts of what was probably a deliberately obscure original Shakespearean *Hamlet* have led some to criticize apparent loose ends within the play. On the other hand, Scofield writes that this play, "more perhaps than any other of Shakespeare's plays, puts us in situations where we have to draw conclusions which are not stated in the play's text. ... A successful criticism of the play would have to keep a constant tension between the speeches and actions that are there before us, and the dimensions behind themselves they must inevitably suggest."[66] Stage directions have been added, omitted, or misplaced; interpretations have been lost, forgotten, or unimagined. *Hamlet* invites the director to see apparent inconsistencies as stage directions embedded in spoken lines. As Mason points out, preparing the play for modern

---

[65]   Johnston, "Introductory Lecture on Shakespeare's *Hamlet*," pt. A.

[66]   Scofield, *The Ghosts of Hamlet*, 161.

playgoers should not result in removing hints, ideas, or indications about interpretation: "[T]hat which has been 'normalised and clarified' has often been drained of shades of interpretive color which we can surely not afford to lose."[67]

Spectators in the early 1600s witness deception, betrayal, witchcraft, and disease with a more modern, turn of the century awareness. As stated earlier, my interpretation does not eliminate characters or story lines from Shakespeare's play and is imagined from the spoken lines of the early texts. The following topics are offered in support of this interpretation:

1. Shakespeare's England
2. Shakespeare's ghost and powers of illusion
3. Staging ideas
4. Conclusion
5. Appendices: Timeline, Sources

---

[67]   Pamela Mason, "'… and Laertes': The Case against Tidiness," in *Stage Directions in "Hamlet,"* ed. Aasand, 98.

CHAPTER TWO:

SHAKESPEARE'S ENGLAND and THE VERY AGE AND BODY OF THE TIME

S ome conclude that Shakespeare's *Hamlet*, "full of gorgeous poetry and profound flashes of insight, is dramatically a thing of shreds and patches."[68] But political risks may have led to an intentionally patchy script. These risks are considered here. A director would want to closely consider what the writer's dramatic intent would have been given the eventful years around the turn of the century. Wilson says it well: "[T]he life at the courts of Elizabeth and James, the persons and doings of the great men of the land, the political and social events of the hour—these form the real background of his plays."[69] What reactions to *Hamlet* would Shakespeare have anticipated from contemporaries? To better understand the more complex and integrated roles for Horatio, Fortinbras, and the ghost, we will consider some of the political, religious, and social stresses pressing on turn of the sixteenth century England.

Some influential relationships among powerful contemporaries would have been known to Shakespeare: William Cecil (Lord Burghley after

---

[68]   Wilson, *What Happens in "Hamlet,"* 14.

[69]   Wilson, *The Essential Shakespeare*, 13.

1571), the queen's chief adviser; Queen Elizabeth I; John Dee, court astrologer and mathematician; Francis Walsingham, head of the spy service; the Earl of Essex, a distinguished courtier, soldier, and candidate to succeed Queen Elizabeth I; the Earl of Southampton, friend of Essex and patron of William Shakespeare; Robert Cecil, William's son and successor; King James I (James VI of Scotland), successor to Queen Elizabeth I; Mary Queen of Scots, James's Catholic mother and perceived rival to the Protestant Elizabeth; and Francis Bacon, nephew to William Cecil, cousin to Robert Cecil and friend to Essex. Volumes have been written about these historical heavyweights, and the scope of this work allows only a brief glance at them. That glance is intended to create an image of England in transition from the medieval worldview to early modern Europe, and to encourage the reader to select biographical sources for further research into Shakespeare's time. It is fascinating reading.

What is in the mirror Shakespeare would hold up to show us "the very age and body of the time, his form, and pressure" (III.ii.)? During the Reformation and Renaissance of early modern Europe, long-standing religious beliefs and dogma came into question. People were sharply divided along religious lines, and the struggle between Catholics and Protestants proved dangerous and deadly. England's Protestant Queen Elizabeth was charged with being a "servant of infamy" by the Pope, while the Protestant head of England's spy service referred to Catholic Mary Queen of Scots as a "devilish woman" who had to be destroyed.

The mirror also began to reveal the fallibilities of superstition or magic to explain events. Observable, predictable (we now say "scientific") explanations were coming into sharper focus. People were beginning to accept argument and reason, but it required an educated effort to refrain from assigning supernatural or dogmatic causes for events where natural causes were yet unknown. Learning and discoveries eclipsed medieval certainties. With *Hamlet*, Shakespeare positions grasp bars of modernity to aid contemporaries in free fall from medieval ways of life and understanding.

Governments were developing more secretive and sophisticated methods for obtaining and using information. England, under William Cecil, developed a network of spying and intelligence services. Their task was said to be to protect Protestant Elizabeth from enemies such as Catholics, who might plot to replace her with a Catholic. These spy agencies would benefit from instruction in the latest techniques of controlling, gathering, and disseminating information; sometimes they used disinformation and torture to produce the desired results. The relatively new printing press technology, which brought an explosion of information to the reading public, could be exploited to disseminate false and slanderous information.

See this book's first appendix for an abbreviated timeline of events leading to the printing of *Hamlet*. This timeline is a recipe for a stew of political intrigue.

WITCHCRAFT VERSUS "DISCOVERIE"

Many in Shakespeare's time believed the power of evil spirits (witchcraft) could be used against people. The Englishmen John Dee (1527-1608) and Reginald Scot (ca. 1538-1599) challenged medieval beliefs in magic and witchcraft. Their works sought natural or scientific explanations for magic and witchcraft, thus putting them on the cutting edge of modern Elizabethan learning and culture. Shakespeare would have been familiar with some of their works.

John Dee, astronomer, mathematician, and technical adviser for espionage, brought the advancement of science and the charm and power of illusion to the courts of Henry VIII's successor Tudor children (Edward, Mary, and Elizabeth).[70] He wrote the preface to the English translation of Euclid's *Elements* (1570). He possessed manuscripts, apparatus for experiments, and a library with significant works about alchemy, demonology, and the occult. During the Renaissance, there was enthusiastic study of the science of optics and the production of artificial specters. Dee addresses the production of images seen in the air by means of perspective glasses. From optics, he passes on to mechanics, describing several topics including a strange "self-moving" metal head, which seemed to speak.[71] (Perhaps Dee also knew of the robotic knight in full German armor that Leonardo da Vinci created a century before Shakespeare's *Hamlet*.) As a young student at Cambridge and decades before Shakespeare's plays, Dee stage-managed a student theatre production wherein a giant mechanical beetle appeared to fly on its own. This shocking spectacle was enough to spread rumors that he possessed supernatural powers.

John Dee influenced the lives of royals and heads of state. He calculated horoscopes for both young Queens Mary (Tudor) and Elizabeth. As court mathematician

---

[70] Some of the biographical information about John Dee is from Charlotte Fell Smith's *John Dee, 1527-1608* (London: Constable, 1909).

[71] Fell Smith, *John Dee*, 26.

and astrologer, Dee instructed King Edward and Queens Mary and Elizabeth. Early on, Dee gained an introduction to William Cecil and likely taught Cecil's children and wards. Dee also coached Elizabethan England's two most powerful men, William Cecil (Burghley) and Francis Walsingham, in spy techniques. William Cecil served Queen Elizabeth throughout most of her reign, at various times as Secretary of State, founder and head of her spy service, Master of the Court of Wards, and Lord Treasurer. He was knighted by Elizabeth's brother, Edward VI, in 1551, and Elizabeth elevated William Cecil to Baron Burghley in 1571.

Dee gained an introduction to Cecil through the scholar John Cheke. William Cecil's first wife and the mother of his son Thomas, was John Cheke's sister.[72] Alan Haynes writes, "In 1552 Girolamo Cardano (Cardanus) was in London staying with Sir John Cheke ... It is known that Cardano met John Dee at Cheke's home."[73] Cardano devised the Cardan grille — a pierced device to aid in sending coded messages. He also described a *camera obscura* with a convex lens to project a clearer image (*De Subtilitate*, 1550).

John Dee was also friend and neighbor to Walsingham, who succeeded Burghley (William Cecil) as head of the spy service. Dee's studies in science and the art of illusion led him to instruct both Burghley and Walsingham in the use of ciphers. Dee was like a skilled

---

[72]   Sir John Cheke was a learned scholar and leader of the Protestant cause in England. He was William's brother-in-law and Thomas's uncle. He advanced and prospered under his pupil King Edward, but when (Catholic) Mary came to the throne he fled England. He was captured and returned to the Tower in London where he began a lengthy, humiliating recantation of his Protestant beliefs. He was released and died about a year later.

[73]   Haynes, *Invisible Power*, 18.

chef to the appetites of Elizabeth's spymasters, William Cecil (Burghley) and later Francis Walsingham. Cecil had studied cryptography and although both men knew the importance of cryptography and optical effects, their loyalties to Dee could wane. Perhaps they feared their ability to control him. Burghley sent spies to watch Dee when he was traveling on the continent. Dee wrote to Walsingham from abroad, and it is probable that Dee himself was acting as a spy and sending encoded messages back to Walsingham.

Abilities in mathematics and optics also put Dee in danger. In the early years of Queen Elizabeth's reign (1563), an Act of Parliament decreed that all who practiced sorcery causing death should die and that those who practiced sorcery causing only injury should be imprisoned and pilloried: "Any conjuration of an evil spirit was to be punished by death as a felon, without benefit of clergy or sanctuary."[74] Would Dee have feared this could apply to his experiments in optics? Would Shakespeare have feared this could apply to his theater productions?

By the 1590s, when Shakespeare was considering the themes in *Hamlet*, Dee was being persecuted for being in league with the devil. Those who studied nature's laws or made calculations and projections about life through geometry and observing the planets seemed diabolically clever to some people. Elizabeth respected Dee and shielded him from those who, by reason of his studies, would seek to overthrow him.

In the 1590s hundreds of "witches" were put to death. Dee believed those accused of witchcraft, whose brains were disordered by melancholy, merited pity, not

---

[74]   Fell Smith, *John Dee*, 61.

punishment. Joining Dee in defending those accused of witchcraft, is the author Reginald Scot, who writes:

> Witchcraft is in truth a cousening [cozening or conjuring] art, wherin the name of God is abused, prophaned and blasphemed and his power attributed to a vile creature. In estimation of the vulgar people, it is a supernaturall worke, contrived between a corporall old woman, and a spirituall divell. The manner thereof is so ... strange, that to this daie there hath never beene any credible witnes therof. It is incomprehensible to the wise, learned or faithful; a probable matter to children, fooles, melancholike persons and papists. ... The effect and end thereof to be sometimes evill, as when thereby man or beast ... is hurt: sometimes good, as whereby sicke folks are healed ... and true men come to their goods. ... The mater and instruments, wherewith it is accomplished, are words, charmes, signes, images, characters.[75]

John Dee, in turn, would defend Scot's *Discoverie of Witchcraft,*[76] a book uncovering or revealing cozening (magic) as nothing more than illusion, sleight of hand, or the knavery and confederacy of conspiring agents. Scot argues that "magic" or "witchcraft" is the manipulation of conditions of perception — not supernatural powers. Scot also describes the invalidity of forced confessions from old women accused of witchcraft. These were intimidated by authorities, "constrained by force, compelled by fear," and "deceived by ignorance."[77] Scot's *Discoverie of Witchcraft* is recognized as one of Shakespeare's source books.[78] Beliefs in evil spirits, witchcraft, and sorcery stemmed from pagan times but

---

[75]   Scot, *Discoverie of Witchcraft,* bk. 16, chap. 2.

[76]   "Discoverie" means the uncovering or revealing. This uncovering of witchcraft meant exposing techniques that would produce illusionary effects.

[77]   Scot, *Discoverie of Witchcraft,* bk. 3, chap. 8.

[78]   Wilson, *What Happens in "Hamlet,"* 63.

were still active in Shakespeare's time, and he would
have been interested in the controversial modern
themes in Scot's book. As a playwright and director,
he would have also been interested in discussions of
illusion to produce stage effects.

Before James became King James I of England (1603),
and while he was still King James VI of Scotland, he
argued against Scot's assertion that spirits do not take
material form. James considered himself an expert on
witches, ghosts, and demons, and had written a book,
Daemonologie, on the subject.[79] James was convinced
of the powers of witchcraft. The king writes "against
the damnable opinions of two principally in our age,
whereof the one called Scot an Englishman, is not
ashamed in publike print to deny, that ther can be such
a thing as Witch-craft ..."[80] In a rather non-Protestant
way, James continues that a ghost or evil spirit can
inhabit a dead body. He holds that a spirit can return
to one who seeks revenge or is evil, that an evil spirit
works easily with a melancholic mind, and that a spirit
may cause madness. Contemporary Protestants would
have accepted the possibility of apparitions, yet it was
not possible that they were spirits of the departed
because the dead went directly to heaven or hell. "The
orthodox Protestant conclusion was that ghosts, while
occasionally they might be angels, were generally
nothing but devils, who 'assumed' ... the form of

---

[79] King James VI, *Daemonologie* (Edinburgh: 1597). James's wife was
Anne of Denmark. The first time she tried to come to Scotland to
marry him, stormy seas forced her ship to turn back. The second time,
James went to Denmark to bring her to Scotland, and again stormy
seas almost caused them to shipwreck. James blamed these bad
storms on witchcraft. When he returned to Scotland, many "witches"
were executed.

[80] Wilson, *What Happens in "Hamlet,"* 64.

departed friends or relatives in order to work bodily or spiritual harm upon those to whom they appeared."[81]

This ghost disagreement was in the forefront of consideration in 1599, while Shakespeare was preparing his version(s) of *Hamlet*.[82] Four years later, and shortly after coming to England's throne, King James ordered Scot's *Discoverie of Witchcraft* burned.

In *What Happens in "Hamlet,"* Wilson summarizes Scot's skeptical views on witchcraft, devils, and spirits. Scot does not contest the existence of spirits; he contests the possibility that they assume material form. "In a word, apparitions are either the illusion of melancholic minds or flat knavery on the part of some rogue. ... [P]ersons subject to melancholy, as Hamlet was, were peculiarly prone to spectral visitations."[83] These statements neatly describe the interpretation offered here: the staging of his dead father's ghost to Hamlet, a person subject to melancholy, is flat knavery. This knavery not only seeks to anonymously coerce the murder of Claudius, but it also pushes Hamlet deeper into instability and melancholy.[84]

After an outbreak of plague and Queen Elizabeth's death in early 1603, London theaters closed. The theaters periodically closed because theater crowds were seen as a means of spreading disease such as

---

[81]   Wilson, *What Happens in "Hamlet,"* 62. We remember here that Hamlet and Horatio have been scholars at the University in Wittenberg where Martin Luther had also been a scholar.

[82]   And see F. W. Moorman's two articles in the *Modern Language Review* 1, no. 6 (1905): "The Pre-Shakespearean Ghost" (85-95), and "Shakespeare's Ghosts" (192-201).

[83]   Wilson, *What Happens in "Hamlet,"* 64.

[84]   The politically powerful "paid for their advantage in nervous debility. There was the oppressive sense of enemies observing every move." Haynes, *Invisible Power*, xiv.

the plague, which took the lives of tens of thousands of Londoners between 1592 and 1603. In 1603, Shakespeare's company left London to go on the road, and they stayed in the small village of Mortlake, the location of Dee's mansion, libraries, and laboratories.

Dee was "famously generous" writes Iain Wright, who believes the playwright and Dee would have known each other.[85] With the loss of Elizabeth, his defender, and the accession of James, his accuser, this would have been a sad and uneasy time for John Dee. It is easy to imagine Dee and Shakespeare eagerly discussing ways to create illusions for the theater, especially if staged illusions altered the king's beliefs about witchcraft.

That same year, it is likely Shakespeare's *Hamlet* was performed at Cambridge and Oxford.[86] Within a year, a version of his *Hamlet* was printed, and King James's Parliament passed a more stringent Act against Witchcraft. The law was expanded to bring death without benefit of clergy to anyone invoking or communicating with evil spirits. Shortly before the act became law, Dee presented himself to King James urging the king to clear Dee "of that horrible and damnable ... [slander] ... in report and Print ... that [Dee] is or hath bin a conjurer or caller or invocator of [devils]."[87] Dee also pleaded with King James to change his opinions about witchcraft. He begged the Parliament to pass an Act against Slander

---

[85] Iain Wright, "All Done with Mirrors: Macbeth's Dagger Discovered," *HEAT 10*, new ser., November 2005, 179-200.

[86] The Q1 title page says it has been performed in London, Cambridge, Oxford and elsewhere, but see pages 21-23 in *Cambridge Introduction to Early English Theatre* by Janette Dillon.

[87] Fell Smith, *John Dee*, 293.

instead of an Act against Witchcraft. The slander of presumed witchcraft had afforded "wicked and cruel pretexts for espionage and terrorism," sending many unfortunates to horrible deaths.[88] But Dee had outlived the support of powerful contemporaries (especially Queen Elizabeth) and could not induce Parliament to heed his petition. Standing by James's dismissal of Dee's petition was Robert Cecil, who, according to Smith, was "the great Burghley's little-minded son," and "lacked almost everything that had made [his father] William Cecil, great, even a great sovereign to serve."[89]

THE CECILS

In addition to deadly disagreements over witchcraft and ghosts described above, the tumultuous decades spanning 1584 to 1604 bled with intrigue, regicide, war, conspiracy, rebellion, and executions. Shakespeare brings these topics to the stage in *Hamlet*. Elsinore's underlying themes of spying, deceit, and mortal danger reflect the political turmoil in the years surrounding Shakespeare's writing of *Hamlet*.

William Cecil (1520-1598) had served in Parliament and by age 30 was already Principal Secretary to (Protestant) King Edward VI. When Edward died, the Protestant Cecil conformed enough to (Catholic) Mary Tudor's five-year reign "to keep his lands and his head."[90] During the short reign of Mary Tudor, some Protestants lost their lands, lives, or both. Some,

---

[88]   Fell Smith, *John Dee*, 295.

[89]   Fell Smith, *John Dee*, 298.

[90]   Stephen Budiansky, *Her Majesty's Spymaster* (New York: Viking Penguin, 2005), 45.

like Francis Walsingham, England's future spymaster, fled abroad. When (Protestant) Elizabeth was crowned (1558), Protestant exiles, Walsingham among them, started returning to England.

William Cecil (elevated to Lord Burghley in 1571) served as Elizabeth's chief adviser throughout all but the last few years of her reign, when his son Robert became chief adviser. The Cecils, diligent officials, wielded considerable power. In a 1585 letter, William defends himself against the phrase, *regnum Cecilianum*, which he writes was used "in a rash and malicious mockry," to describe his service.[91] Though the rich and powerful William Cecil confessed to being Elizabeth's loyal subject and humble servant, "the deeper the modern scholar digs into Elizabethan State Papers, the more Cecil demands scrutiny."[92] Early on, he established an intelligence-gathering agency with the public goal of protecting a Protestant queen from assassination threats, and perhaps with the covert goal of protecting his own wealth and powerful position. Francis Walsingham worked for and later led the spy agency.

About three years into Elizabeth's reign (in 1561), Mary Stuart, Catholic cousin to Queen Elizabeth, returned to Scotland from France as Mary Queen of Scots (MaryQS). She was seen as the greatest threat to Elizabeth's throne. Some considered Elizabeth illegitimate and MaryQS the true heir to England's throne. Cecil sent money to aid Scotland's Protestant rebels against MaryQS. Early in his career,

---

[91] John Strype, *The Annals of the Reformation and Establishment of Religion, ... during Queen Elizabeth's Happy Reign,* vol. 3, pt. 2 (Oxford: Clarendon Press, 1824), 380.

[92] John A. Guy, *Queen of Scots: The True Life of Mary Stuart* (Boston: Houghton Mifflin, 2004), 495.

Walsingham wrote to Cecil: "So long as this devilish woman lives, [Queen Elizabeth would not] continue in quiet possession of the crown ..."[93] Walsingham and Burghley (Cecil) worked for nearly two decades to bring down MaryQS (mother of the future King James I of England).

Walsingham, a Protestant, possessed an intense hatred of Catholic rule. He had witnessed the St. Bartholomew's Day Massacre of Protestants in Paris (1572) when a large number of Protestants were in the Catholic city for a royal wedding. France's Catherine de Medici plotted the assassination of some Protestant leaders, and the slaughter of thousands of Protestants followed. Years earlier, MaryQS had been a young member in the household of that ruling Catholic family in France.

Walsingham recruited students from Oxford and Cambridge to train them in intelligence techniques. His trainees could reseal documents, decipher, and forge codes. History credits this spy agency with protecting Elizabeth from plots against her life. Results also appear to credit this spy agency with keeping non royals in powerful positions. (In *Hamlet*, Horatio also gains power.) In 1573, Elizabeth appointed Walsingham Principal Secretary, replacing Burghley, and naming Burghley Lord Treasurer. Walsingham also headed the spy agency.

Mary Queen of Scots lived an extraordinarily eventful and tragic life (1542-1587). The historian William Camden claims she was one among princesses who "have changed their Felicity for Misery and Calamity."[94]

---

[93]   Budiansky, *Her Majesty's Spymaster*, 81.

[94]   William Camden, *The History of the Most Renowned and Victorious Princess Elizabeth, Late of England: Selected Chapters*, ed. Wallace T.

Mary was daughter to James V of Scotland and Mary Guise of France, and great-granddaughter to Elizabeth's grandfather, England's Henry VII. Mary's father died when she was six days old, and she was named Queen of Scots. Five years later, for her protection, she was sent to live with the French royal family. At age fifteen, she married Francis, the heir to the French throne and less than a year later, Mary's husband became King. Attending his coronation were Mary's future husbands, Henry Stuart (Lord Darnley) and James Hepburn (Earl of Bothwell). The young King of France died shortly after becoming king. Eerily similar to the ghost's story of old Hamlet, Francis died after falling ill with a middle ear inflammation that spread to his brain.

A charming, devoutly Catholic eighteen-year-old Mary returned to Scotland as queen, but she was not easily accepted by Scotland's Protestant Lords of the Congregation who were already ruling Scotland and enjoying privileges of the court. Mary's illegitimate half-brother, James Stewart, 1st Earl of Moray (or Murray), also a descendent of Henry VII, was a leader of the Lords of the Congregation. About four years before Mary's return, these Lords had banded together to "forsake and renounce the congregation of Satan" (the Roman Catholic Church) and proclaimed Scotland a Protestant land. Cecil favored the Earl of Moray, but saw Mary as a threat to Elizabeth, and he helped Mary's adversaries. Before Mary's return to Scotland, Moray went to visit her in France. On his way to France, he first consulted with Elizabeth and Cecil in

MacCaffrey (Chicago: University of Chicago Press, 1970), 288. Also see xxiv for information about when this quote was written and Camden's demand that the work not be published in his lifetime.

England. Once in France, Morey urged Mary to become Protestant. Mary suggested he become Catholic. They could not agree to be of one religion but did agree that when Mary returned to Scotland, she could continue to worship as Catholic and "would not interfere with the Protestant church."[95] Mass was illegal in Scotland, but Mary was allowed a private mass. This angered Protestants, most vehemently, John Knox, a leader in Scotland's reformation.

Perhaps unwisely, MaryQS married Henry Stuart (Lord Darnley).[96] Related to both Queens Elizabeth and Mary, he was, like Mary, a great-grandchild to Henry VII. Compellingly handsome at first, Darnley became rude, reckless, overbearing, and generally unlikeable. He was often ill and was treated for syphilis. During this marriage, Mary became pregnant with James, the future king of both Scotland and England.

Mary enjoyed the company of her Italian secretary, David Rizzio. Some lords convinced Darnley that Rizzio was acting not only as Mary's secretary, but also as her lover. They hatched a plot to kill Rizzio. The murderers took no consideration for protecting Mary's pregnancy; on the contrary, they may have wanted to force her to miscarry. One evening (1566) while she was having supper with a small group including Rizzio, Darnley entered the room. Then a Lord Ruthven, dressed in complete armor, appeared at her door and demanded Rizzio come with him. When Mary refused to allow this, several men entered, and there in her presence, they viciously stabbed her friend Rizzio to death. The extent to which Cecil

---

[95]   Rosalind K. Marshall, *Elizabeth I* (Owings Mills, MD: Stemmer, 1991), 80.

[96]   Henry Stuart or Stewart, cousin to MaryQS.

orchestrated Rizzio's murder may never be known, but his agents kept him well informed of the plot even before the murder took place.

Mary was much shaken. She was angry at her husband's part in her friend's murder, but she must have convinced Darnley that it had been a mistake to trust these men and participate in the murder. Within days, Mary and Darnley managed to slip away from castle guards and join the Earl of Bothwell, whose army escorted them back to Edinburgh.[97] This of course angered the Scottish lords. A few months later, the baby James was born, and Mary and Darnley seemed on better terms.

Less than a year after the birth of James, Darnley was murdered (1567). Evidence points to the murder being a conspiracy among several men. Few people, enemy or friend of Mary, liked Darnley. This crime widened an opening for slander and more secret operations against Mary. Only days after Darnley's death, posters appeared accusing Mary and Bothwell of immoral acts, and so began an intense campaign to slander Mary and Bothwell, who were presumed to be lovers. Historians differ on the reality of their love for each other, but none deny the tragedy of their relationship. They were accused of planning the murder. To establish their guilt before trial, rumors were spread through anonymous posters, pamphlets, and graffiti. Even voices in the night claimed that Mary and Bothwell had killed Darnley:

> On the night following [Darnley's] funeral the profound silence of Edinburgh was broken by a long shrill cry, as of a

---

[97]   James Hepburn, 4th Earl of Bothwell and Lord High Admiral of Scotland, was consistently loyal to Mary and to Mary's mother, the queen regent. He intercepted moneys sent from Cecil intended to support the Scottish Lords' efforts against the Scots crown.

wandering man. Several people heard him, and shivered in their beds; only one, bolder than the rest saw him in a broad patch of moonlight. He came ... flap-hatted and cloaked; and as he went now and again he threw his head towards the moon, and cried, like one called the news, "Vengeance on those who caused me to shed innocent blood! O Lord, open the heavens and pour down vengeance on those that have destroyed the innocent!" Upon the hushed city the effect was terrible ... no windows were opened and no watchman ventured to stop the man. But next morning there was found a bill upon the Cross which accused Bothwell by name of the deed. It drew a crowd, and then ... all tongues were loosened and all pens set free to rail. The Queen was not spared; pictures of her as the Siren, fish-tailed, ogling, naked ... made the walls shameful. The preachers took up the text and shrieked her name; and every night the shrouded crier went his rounds.[98]

Bothwell was brought to trial for the murder of Darnley. He still had some political pull and by mid-April was acquitted of the murder. Several days later, after obtaining written permission (the Ainslie Bond) from about 30 nobles and bishops to marry Mary, he abducted her, took her to his castle, and (by some reports) raped her. Bothwell managed to divorce his wife and by May 15, three months after the Darnley murder, he and Mary were married. This marriage was not well-received — it angered the lords, Queen Elizabeth, Protestants (Mary was Catholic), and the Pope (Bothwell was divorced). Scottish lords again turned against the pair and raised an army to confront them. One month after their marriage, Mary and Bothwell's forces were defeated in their attempt to regain control of Scotland. Propaganda against Mary was strong, and people did not rally behind them as they had hoped. Her army melted away. Bothwell was

---

[98]   Maurice Henry Hewlett, *The Queen's Quair or The Six Years' Tragedy* (New York: Scribner's, 1912), 437.

47

forced to flee Scotland, and Mary was taken prisoner to yet another castle. She was humiliated in front of her subjects. About a month later, after miscarrying twins, she was slandered as a whore and forced to abdicate. This left the crown to her toddler son James and the government to James's (illegitimate) uncle, the Earl of Moray, as regent. Three years later, Moray, by then strongly implicated in Darnley's murder, was himself murdered.[99]

After Bothwell fled Scotland, his ship was captured by pirates, and he was taken to the Danish king whose chancellor, Rosencrantz, recognized him as the man who had abandoned marriage plans to Rosencrantz's cousin. Bothwell, former lover and husband of James's mother, was, at first humanely, later cruelly, imprisoned for breach of contract in Denmark, where he died insane.

For most of her adult life, MaryQS was a prisoner in castles in Scotland or England. She would have understood Hamlet's disgust at being spied upon, his observation that Elsinore is a prison, and his uncertainty about who can be trusted.

Almost twenty years into MaryQS's confinement in England, Walsingham found a way to bring her to trial. He hired a double agent, Gilbert Gifford, to carry her secret correspondence. Mary trusted Gifford and didn't know he was working for Walsingham. Walsingham told Elizabeth he had decoded treasonous messages inside Mary's letters proposing to remove Queen Elizabeth and free Mary. The spy service added forged postscripts to the letter exchange, asking for names. Names were supplied, and those named were brutally executed.

---

[99] Stephen Alford notes this was the "first political killing by firearm in the British Isles." Stephen Alford, *The Watchers: A Secret History of the Reign of Elizabeth I* (London: Penguin, 2013), 133-134.

At her trial, Mary realized that Walsingham had trapped her, but her attacks on him and his intelligence forces failed. She declared she had no plan to harm Elizabeth and she could not speak for what plans others may have had. Walsingham's evidence was at best second-hand. When pressed on the contents of a letter, Mary argued that it would be easy for someone to counterfeit the cipher and handwriting of another. When Mary asked to see the evidence against her, this was denied. When Mary asked for an advocate, Burghley denied her request. When she asked for one more day to prepare a defense, he denied this, too.

Mary was beheaded in 1587.[100] Contemporary historian William Camden wrote cautiously of the trial at Fotheringhay, which took MaryQS's life. He preferred it be "enwrapped up in silence, than once spoken of: Let it be forgotten quite ..." Without naming names, Camden allows that "[u]nder the best Princes some there are who being once armed with authority, know how by secret slights to set a goodly shew and fair pretense of conscience and Religion, thereby to cloke their owne private designes ..."[101]

Burghley and Walsingham owned Mary's story "enwrapped in silence" and "forgotten quite." (Similarly, at play's end, Horatio owns Hamlet's story.) Mary's story cannot be clearly known—each point of evidence is subject to state revision and offered from an

---

[100] At Mary's execution, she put her head on the block. It took two blows for the executioner to sever her head. When the executioner tried to take the head by its hair to show the severance, the head fell away from a wig, revealing short grey hair. Her lips continued moving for several minutes. Her pet dog came out from hiding in her skirts and stood between the head and the body. See Cuthbert Bede (pen name for Edward Bradley), *Fotheringhay and Mary, Queen of Scots* (London: Simpkin, Marshall, 1886), 128-131.

[101] Bede, *Fotheringhay and Mary, Queen of Scots*, 161.

invested or prejudicial point of view. At Walsingham's death (1590), many papers, which could have revealed official misdeeds, went missing. Robert Cecil has been named as the one who took these papers. Guy cautions that Guy's biography of Mary is not Mary's story, "History is written by the winners and ... she was to be a spectacular loser."[102]

Shakespeare and his company of actors would have known of state deceptions and of how the spy service could sway court opinion, force royal decisions, torture, imprison, and execute people. Anonymous propaganda had contributed to Mary's downfall. At her trial, MaryQS observed, "Spies are men of doubtful credit, who make a show of one thing and speak another."[103] Shakespeare repeats Mary's observation in the characters of Horatio, Polonius, Reynaldo, and Voltemand. Polonius urges Laertes to be true to himself (I.iii.) then sends someone to spy on him — "Even catch a carp of truth by a bait of falsehood" (II.i.). Polonius's character could be drawn from the character of Lord Burghley, who received reports about his older son, Thomas, while he was a student in Paris.[104] For Polonius, Reynaldo, and Claudius, there is an obvious and routine acceptance of dishonesty, spying, and eavesdropping. Dishonesty and knavery, even to abuse the weak, were forces in Hamlet's Denmark as well as in the English spy service.

---

[102]   Guy, *Queen of Scots*, 341.

[103]   Bede, *Fotheringhay and Mary, Queen of Scots*, 99.

[104]   "According to intelligence [Burghley] had gathered, Thomas was ... gaining a reputation as a lout ... 'in study soon weary, in game never.'" Mark Anderson, *Shakespeare by Another Name* (New York: Penguin, 2005), 15.

School chums Rosencrantz and Guildenstern are enlisted to spy on Hamlet. Similar to the way Walsingham intercepted and changed Mary's letters, Hamlet alters the text of the letter from Claudius to the authorities in England and reapplies the seal. England accepts this altered letter as genuine, which causes Rosencrantz and Guildenstern, like Mary, to be put to death. England's spy service first under William Cecil (Burghley), then Walsingham, then Robert Cecil, trained in these techniques of deception.

Susan Ronald writes that by the mid-1590s, Burghley's son Robert Cecil (1563-1612) was "the most powerful man in all England."[105] "Effectively [R.] Cecil was now prime minister, home secretary, and foreign minister."[106] He was already serving as Secretary of State in 1598 when his father, Lord Burghley, died.[107] The father had groomed Robert to follow him, and Robert continued on to head the spy agency as well.

Robert had grown up in the Cecil household along with wards of the state whom his father, as Master of the Court of Wards, sponsored. Among these were the Earls of Essex (Robert Devereux), Southampton (Henry Wriothesley), Rutland (Roger Manners), and Oxford (Edward de Vere). Essex's "good looks were astonishing," and he possessed "a quick personal charm," while Robert Cecil was "crippled and graceless

---

[105] Susan Ronald, *Heretic Queen: Queen Elizabeth I and the Wars of Religion* (New York: St. Martin's Press, 2012), 290.

[106] Ronald, *Heretic Queen*, 290.

[107] The year before Burghley's death included the queen's "grand climacteric, that year of utmost significance to those like Dr. Dee who cast horoscopes ..." In 1597, Burghley was sixty-six; the queen was sixty-three, Robert Cecil was thirty-three, the Earl of Essex and King James VI were thirty. P. M. Handover, *The Second Cecil: The Rise of Power 1563-1604 of Sir Robert Cecil, later Earl of Salisbury* (London: Eyre and Spottiswoode, 1959), 151.

in movement, less striking in appearance."[108] Motley describes a young Robert Cecil as "a slight, crooked, hump-backed young gentleman, dwarfish in stature ... with a disposition almost ingenuous, as compared to the massive dissimulation with which it was to be contrasted, and with what was, in after times to constitute a portion of his own character."[109]

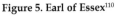

Figure 5. Earl of Essex[110]   **Figure 6. Robert Cecil**[111]

Shakespeare describes deformity using Gloucester's words in *Richard III*, Act I, scene 1:

But I, that am not shap'd for sportive tricks,
Nor made to court an amorous looking-glass;

[108] Handover, *The Second Cecil*, 17.

[109] John Lothrop Motley, *History of the United Netherlands: From the Death of William the Silent to the Twelve Years' Truce – 1609*, vol. 2 (New York: Harper, 1861), 359.

[110] Charles Knight, ed., *Shakspere, a Biography* (London: C. Knight & Co., 1843), 412.

[111] Charles Knight, ed., *Shakspere, a Biography*, 409.

I, that am rudely stamp'd, and want love's majesty
To strut before a wanton ambling nymph;
I, that am curtail'd of this fair proportion,
Cheated of feature by dissembling nature,
Deform'd, unfinish'd, sent before my time
...
And therefore, since I cannot prove a lover,
...
I am determined to prove a villain ...

The Earl of Southampton, a (bravely) declared Catholic, would become Shakespeare's patron. Shakespeare dedicated poems to him in 1593 and 1594. Southampton was a devoted ally of Essex, and stood by him in the failed 1601 rebellion. The Earl of Oxford (Edward de Vere) would marry Burghley's daughter (Robert's sister, Thomas's half-sister), Anne, and serve in official capacity at the trials of MaryQS and of the Earls of Essex and Southampton.

There were several contemporary, tragic personalities for Shakespeare's sketchbook of *Hamlet* characters. This writing very briefly views several of these personalities, but it leaves out several important ones, among them Thomas Kyd, Christopher Marlowe, Thomas Howard (Duke of Norfolk), Anthony Babington, John Story, and Henry Cuffe.

Wilson believes Shakespeare drew heavily from the character of the Earl of Essex (1566-1601) to inform the character of Hamlet. He writes, "Hamlet is not Essex; he is Shakespeare's effort to understand Essex."[112] This handsome courtier was thirty-some years younger than Elizabeth, had been a favorite of the queen and court,

---

[112]   Wilson, *The Essential Shakespeare*, 104. And from page 107, "... for his contemporaries, [*Hamlet*] served as a revelation of the troubled spirit of the most puzzling and the most canvassed character of the time."

and was commonly viewed as a likely successor to his distant (Boleyn) relative, the childless Queen Elizabeth.

Perhaps in an attempt to gain more favor with Queen Elizabeth, Essex nurtured a weakly substantiated plot to convict the queen's doctor of treason. Common law forbade torture, but the Privy Council would put this law aside if it could lead to identifying [real or imagined] plots against the queen.[113] Torture was used to extract the desired information — if the person refused to confess, it was not seen as innocence, but as a need for more torture. The doctor admitted guilt only under extreme torture, and was executed. The old doctor "was strung up, cut down while still living, castrated, disembowelled and cut in four."[114]

In the four or so years before Essex's own execution, his impetuous actions and Robert Cecil's steady, tightening control managed to undo Essex's chances at succession. When Burghley died in 1598, court loyalties split between the Earl of Essex and Robert Cecil. Like his father before him, Robert Cecil was too clever, hard-working, dug-in, and adept at the daily business of state to be replaced by the passionate, well-liked, but outspoken and often erratic Earl of Essex. Cecil was always a calculated step ahead of Essex.[115]

Essex had given considerable time, company, and military service to the aging queen and was exasperated that her favor went increasingly Robert Cecil's way. While Essex was in Ireland, she had appointed Cecil the new Master of Wards, a lucrative position Essex expected for himself. So while Essex was in poor health

---

[113] Haynes, *Invisible Power*, 50.

[114] Robert Lacey, *Robert, Earl of Essex: An Elizabethan Icarus* (London: Weidenfeld and Nicolson, 1971), 120.

[115] And see Handover, *The Second Cecil*, 144.

and slogging it out in Ireland fighting for the queen, Cecil attained great powers and now led as Secretary of State [Principal Secretary], spymaster, Master of Wards, and information chief. As chief of information, he established a comprehensive news service and was "the first to define 'news' in parliament ... The word itself was new. ... The custody of the news, like the custody of the signet seal, was what gave unassailable power to the Principal Secretary."[116]

Essex tried to achieve success and advancement playing by the old rules and felt thwarted by Cecil. While Essex's military successes were cheered by the people and grandly feted at court, these became less important than Cecil's steady day-to-day management of affairs of state. This contrast can also be seen in the first and last duel presented in *Hamlet*. The first duel, man-to-man between kings (old Hamlet and old Fortinbras), was, as Jan Blits writes, "a contest of the medieval warrior virtue in which duelists fought to the death armed with their weapons and their courage." The duel between Laertes and Hamlet, "a defective duplicate, is a contest of Renaissance gentlemanly skill, in which duelists, risking not their lives but their 'shame and odd hits' [V.ii. 158], entertain the court by fighting against each other to beat the point spread. ... Fortune, skill, and entertainment have replaced courage, chivalry, and death."[117] Charles Knight quotes Queen Elizabeth in this regard, "Speaking of the days of her ancestors, she said— 'In those days force and arms did prevail, but now the wit of the fox is everywhere on foot, so as hardly a faithful or virtuous man may be found.'"[118]

---

[116]   Handover, *The Second Cecil*, 271.

[117]   Blits, *Deadly Thought*, 364.

[118]   Charles Knight, ed., *Shakspere, a Biography*, 411.

Events in Essex's final years would have drawn the playwright's attention. The Earl of Essex had a magnetic personality. While favorite to the queen, he secretly wooed and later married Walsingham's daughter. He could also be subject to bouts of melancholy and indecision. Depths of religious melancholy offset bouts of tragically erratic excitements. Contemporaries doubted his mental stability. His friend Francis Bacon asked him why he thought the queen would let him manage her affairs when he couldn't even manage his own.[119] Essex was also rumored to have syphilis. Robert Lacey writes that "[h]is behaviour had been growing more and more erratic in the course of the last years, and tertiary syphilis seems a plausible clinical explanation ... The final three months of Essex's life were a confused jumble of fears, rages, sly plottings and crude irrational outbursts of emotion, culminating in the tragic and dismal ... February rebellion."[120]

After leading a failed military expedition to Ireland and behaving rashly toward Elizabeth, Essex was held under house arrest and banned from court (1599). Lacey Baldwin Smith notes that while Essex was under house arrest, "[t]here is considerable evidence of a network of spies in Essex's household. ... [O]ne of Essex's complaints ... was that they 'laid his own servants spies to entrap him.'"[121] Essex believed Elizabeth was surrounded by evil counselors. In 1601, while still banned from court and in secret negotiations with James VI of Scotland concerning Elizabeth's successor, the Earl of Essex led a rebellion against evil counselors surrounding Queen Elizabeth.

[119]   Lacey, *Robert, Earl of Essex*, 172.

[120]   Lacey, *Robert, Earl of Essex*, 261-262.

[121]   Smith, *Treason in Tudor England*, 315.

On February 7, the afternoon before the rebellion, Shakespeare's players performed *Richard II* in the Globe theater for the Essex party; Essex had seen several performances of it. In this play, which had been censored at court, the king is deposed. Played before the Essex faction, the play was intended to stir people to join the rebellion.[122] That same night, Queen Elizabeth asked the Privy Council to investigate this performance.[123] Shakespeare's company, the Chamberlain's Men, was asked to explain why they had staged *Richard II*. The patron of the Chamberlain's Men was George Carey, relative to both Queen Elizabeth and the Earl of Essex through Mary Boleyn, Elizabeth's aunt. The company received only a reprimand, but this attempt to control the theater likely troubled Shakespeare. Shakespeare probably worked on his *Hamlet* in the months following the reprimand.[124]

Essex said he wished to save the queen and the crown from her enemies, but the Essex rebellion never gained the anticipated following and failed miserably. Elizabeth and her advisers were well aware of the anticipated rebellion; the queen's heralds, under the leadership of Thomas Cecil, took to the streets early

---

[122] "[M]embers of the Essex party ... induced Shakespeare's company to give a performance of *Richard II* ... At the subsequent trial, the whole story came out, and for a time things looked black for the Globe and its company." Wilson, *The Essential Shakespeare*, 102-103.

[123] Alan Haynes, *Robert Cecil, 1st Earl of Salisbury* (London: Peter Owen Publishers, 1989), 63.

[124] This book views the Cecils as they relate to themes in Shakespeare's *Hamlet*, and I believe Shakespeare was sympathetic to the Essex faction. Shakespeare's patron, Southampton, was Essex's loyal supporter, and on the night before the Essex rebellion, Shakespeare's acting company risked performing *Richard II* when the Essex faction requested this. For a thorough, well-written account of Essex and court politics, see Janet Dickinson's *Court Politics and the Earl of Essex, 1589-1601* (London: Pickering and Chatto, 2012).

proclaiming Essex a traitor and offering a pardon to those who would desert him.[125] Essex's anticipated support quickly slipped away. In despair, Essex returned to his house where he was arrested. The proclamation of Essex's treason announced on that Sunday was printed on Monday and distributed on Tuesday. Essex and Southampton were quickly tried and found guilty. [126]

At the trial, Burghley, though dead, maintained a presence through his sons Thomas and Robert Cecil; his nephew, Francis Bacon; Edward Coke,[127] Attorney-General and lead prosecutor; and at least these former wards — the Earls of Oxford, Essex, Southampton, and Rutland.

Dressed all in black to appear before the court, Essex testified that Robert Cecil had secretly negotiated with Spain regarding the succession of the English crown. Like Polonius in the queen's closet scene (III.iv.), Robert Cecil was hiding behind a court tapestry listening to what Essex said. While Essex was pleading his case, Cecil stepped out from behind the tapestry. With soothing words to the court, he proceeded to destroy Essex's argument:

> My Lord of Essex, the difference between you and me is great ... For wit I give you the pre-eminence — you have it abundantly. For nobility also I give you place — I am not

---

[125]   Lacey, *Robert, Earl of Essex*, 291.

[126]   Sir Henry Neville, also implicated in the rebellion, and the Earl of Southampton were released after James became King of England in 1603.

[127]   Edward Coke was married to Elizabeth Hatton, the (widowed) daughter of Thomas Cecil. Coke and Francis Bacon had competed for the hand of E. Hatton and for the position of Attorney General. Years earlier, Essex had pleaded with the queen to appoint Bacon Attorney General, but at Burghley and R. Cecil's urging, she appointed Coke.

58

noble, yet a gentleman; I am no swordsman—there also
you have the odds; but I have innocence, conscience, truth
and honesty to defend me against the scandal and sting of
slanderous tongues, and in this Court I stand as an upright
man, and your lordship as a delinquent.[128]

Francis Bacon, Essex's onetime friend and confidant,
now sat as counselor to the law on the bench that would
find Essex guilty. Bacon, reluctantly one of Essex's chief
accusers, could color in shades of the betrayed trust
imagined for Horatio.[129] ("The great man down, you
mark his favourite flies, ..." [III.ii.].) Bacon reasoned
that Essex had been steadily losing control, but the
rebellion had gone too far. On the night of 24 February
1601, Shakespeare's company performed at court. The
next morning, the handsome, befuddled head of Essex
rolled from the chopping block.

The execution of Essex was unpopular. The
government needed to quickly publish its account of the
earl's treasons to better frame and publicize the desired
narrative. That Essex had been Bacon's friend and
benefactor was no secret to Queen Elizabeth, but she
ordered Francis Bacon to write the official government
account of the trial anyway. Bacon felt duty-bound to
obey the queen, and this would "lead him to blacken
his friend's character after his death, by garbling with
his own hand the depositions against the victim of his
faction, and publishing them as authentic records of

---

[128] Lacey, *Robert, Earl of Essex*, 307.

[129] Haynes offers a different, more favorable view of Horatio and writes
       that Essex's "calamity led Shakespeare to invent a friend for Hamlet, in
       the play most freighted by those terrifying events, who is the opposite
       of the agitators who clustered about Essex. Horatio represents that
       admirable person—the loyal, steadfast, tactful and virtually silent
       friend." See Haynes, *Invisible Power*, xiv.

the trial."[130] These were published as *A Declaration of the Practices and Treasons [of] ... the Late Earl of Essex.* Bacon waited until Elizabeth died, then in 1604 wrote a letter of apology for the declaration of Essex's treasons, saying the queen and her counselors had so censored and altered his *Declaration* that the result was almost a new writing. Bacon's *Apologie* was later published in 1642 as *His Apologie in certaine imputations concerning the late Earle of Essex.*

In the months following the beheading, hundreds of additional guards were assigned to keep order in the city and among the playhouses and beer gardens. Robert Cecil and the Privy Council were creating story lines to defame Essex and his associates. They wrote history casting Henry Cuffe, Essex's secretary, as an evil scholar who had led Essex to treason and "embarrassed the government and its Queen."[131]

The government also gave preachers instructions for sermons that would relay the story that the Earl of Essex had courted popularity in order to make himself king and that Essex had hypocritically attended church while plotting the downfall of the queen. Even Essex's funeral sermon was dictated by Cecil, and as Alexandra Gajda writes, the privy council "energetically enshrined their official narrative of Essex's treasons from press and pulpit."[132]

Essex's elimination as a contender for the crown secured a future king (James) who would advance Robert Cecil's own political powers. In the play, Claudius is eliminated, and this death secures a king

---

[130] Charles Knight, ed., *Shakspere, a Biography*, 408.

[131] Smith, *Treason in Tudor England*, 253-254.

[132] Alexandra Gajda, *The Earl of Essex and Late Elizabethan Political Culture* (New York: Oxford University Press, 2012), 45.

(Fortinbras) who advances Horatio's position. James had earlier shown support for the Essex faction. When he heard of the rebellion's debacle, he was very concerned that Robert Cecil not find the Essex-James letter exchange. Cecil had not supported James at first, but after Essex's downfall, he entered into a secret understanding with James that James would succeed Elizabeth. Cecil and James VI would seem an unlikely alliance. Cecil's father, Lord Burghley, had been behind the execution of James's mother, MaryQS. "Robert Cecil, of course, prospered, stage-managing the transfer of power from Elizabeth to James in 1603 ... and winning for himself as James's chief minister, the Earldom of Salisbury..."[133] Robert Cecil, like Horatio, is a link between two crowns.[134] James VI, like Fortinbras, offspring of a former enemy, becomes king.

As with MaryQS and Essex, death takes the voice from Hamlet that could tell his story. But Shakespeare could cast Horatio to mirror both Robert Cecil and Francis Bacon as political benefactors and surviving historians. The Earl of Essex, like Hamlet, is an example of a once likeable but increasingly unstable man, teetering on the edge of ruling a kingdom.[135] This comparison of Hamlet to the Earl of Essex, influenced by Wilson's *The Essential Shakespeare*, is one example of numerous attempts to identify historical figures with fictional characters in *Hamlet*. It would have been less creative theatrically and too dangerous politically

---

[133] Lacey, *Robert, Earl of Essex*, 317.

[134] Charlotte Fell Smith determines that Shakespeare's Fortinbras can be none other than James VI of Scotland, who, with Robert Cecil's alliance, succeeded Elizabeth to become James I of England.

[135] "Th'expectancy and rose of the fair state ... Th'observed of all observers, quite, quite down!" (III.i.).

to clearly identify a character in *Hamlet* with a single contemporary of Shakespeare. Shakespeare's theater "newsreel" would have splices and voice-overs; character traits and tragedies are drawn from several contemporaries and spread among various characters in the play.

Elizabeth reigned for forty-five years. The Cecils served as chief advisers to the crown for a combined span of about sixty years. Many met their deaths through strong-armed tactics to ensure her reign. Two famous death sentences, those of MaryQS and the Earl of Essex, are offered here as examples of what Shakespeare would have witnessed in his lifetime. Highlighted in these tragedies are the intrigue, cruelty, slander, and duplicity permeating Shakespeare's England, particularly during his attention to *The Tragedy of Hamlet, Prince of Denmark.*

CHAPTER THREE:

THE POWER OF "AIERIE IMAGES"

T his book's earlier emphasis on the contributions of Scot and Dee to the field of optics and illusion provides some background for the deceptions, changing perspectives, and mortal dangers strongly affecting the court and monarchy in Shakespeare's lifetime. Links between Shakespeare, Scot, and Dee provide "evidence of Shakespeare's direct acquaintance with the discourses of Natural Magic, which were playing a major role in the growth of the modern scientific world view."[136] Reginald Scot's *The Discoverie of Witchcraft* is recognized as one of Shakespeare's sources.[137] Scot defended conjuring as "un-magicking" the world for the simple and asserted conjuring for entertainment and laid bare as illusion is not only not wrong, but is also praiseworthy. As mathematician, court astrologer, and spy consultant, Dee had personal reasons to defend science from sorcery and deceit. Like other "sorcerers" of his day, he was under constant threat of arrest and imprisonment. The play's ghost is added here to the partnership of John Dee and Reginald Scot in common cause "to convince people that many reported apparitions are not demonic in origin but

---

[136]   Wright, "All Done with Mirrors," 197.

[137]   Wilson, *What Happens in "Hamlet,"* 63. (Scot's *Discoverie* was written in 1584.)

have 'natural' — we would say 'scientific' — causes ...
and that it is an affront to our reason not to investigate
and understand them."[138]

FOUL DEEDS WILL RISE

After Essex's unsuccessful military expedition to
Ireland ended in confinement at York House (1599),
Shakespeare worked on his own *Hamlet*. A printed copy
(Q1) appeared about two years after Essex's execution
and during the year of transition from Elizabeth to
James (1603-04). Elizabethans, already schooled in
the Protestant disavowal of ghosts (unless they be
devils masquerading as spirits), were also hearing
from learned scholars about scientific explanations for
magic, witchcraft, and ghosts — be they specters, spirits,
apparitions, or illusions. Emerging and expanding
scientific explanations of the supernatural could
threaten those in power. While the more educated
would not favor supernatural explanations, others
would still cling to a pagan or medieval belief in ghosts.
Still others would be left in uncomfortable uncertainty.

Confrontations with ghosts also occur in
Shakespeare's *Julius Caesar*, *Macbeth*, and *Richard III*.
But in *Hamlet*, Shakespeare's most modern play, the
ghost embodies in one character the evolving tensions
of the age: science vs. sorcery, superstition vs. religion,
Protestantism vs. Catholicism, autonomy vs. coercion,
justice vs. state-sanctioned deception, and regicide/
intrigue vs. peaceful monarchy. Shakespeare uses these
tensions and clashing views to create interest in the
central character of Hamlet, the melancholy Wittenberg
student. The ghost reveals how the powerful abuse the

---

[138]   Wright, "All Done with Mirrors," 181.

questioning and unquestioning alike through trickery and deceit. Governments embrace deceit and illusion as a means to maintain control. When tyrants "were unable or unwilling to found their sovereignty on the affections and interests of their people, they sought to entrench themselves in the strongholds of supernatural influence, and to rule with the delegated authority of heaven. The prince, the priest, and the sage were leagued in a dark conspiracy to deceive and enslave their species..."[139]

In just three decades before Shakespeare's birth in 1564, the country painfully transitioned from Catholic to Protestant to Catholic to Protestant. Hamlet's university in Wittenberg is where Martin Luther's challenges to the Roman Catholic Church launched the Reformation (1517). In 1521, England's Henry VIII attacked Luther and was honored by the Pope as "Defender of Faith." Twelve years later, after his first divorce, Henry VIII broke with the church in Rome and established the Church of England. Among substantial changes ushered in under the protectorate of his successor (nine-year-old son, Edward VI, 1547-1553), were the elimination of the Mass, purgatory, the saints, ornamentation (idols), fasts, and feasts. The successor to Edward (and Lady Jane Grey) was the Catholic Mary Tudor who quickly reestablished the Catholic Mass and rituals (1553). Five years later, she was succeeded by the Protestant Elizabeth who again renounced papal authority. Few of Shakespeare's contemporaries were spared the disruptions and (sometimes mortal) losses these shifts in religion caused. By Shakespeare's time, survivors

---

[139]   David Brewster, *Letters on Natural Magic, Addressed to Sir Walter Scott* (London: John Murray, 1832), 3.

had learned to keep religious feelings to themselves or communicate them in subtle, coded ways.

Although the theater was "full of apparitions and optical illusions,"[140] conflicting religious views of the afterlife and spirits would weigh heavily and perhaps dangerously on theater productions in Elizabethan-Jacobean times. Spectators would include declared Catholics, secret Catholics, and the majority would be declared Protestants. Catholics believed apparitions might be spirits of the dead returned from purgatory to ask assistance in moving from purgatory to heaven. (The ghost in question is not from purgatory because the requested task of murder would not lift the "poor ghost" from purgatory to heaven, although it might bring him Hamlet's company in hell.) Protestants believed in apparitions but did not believe these were spirits of the dead; these were usually "devils" who assumed the form of the dead to work mischief.[141] Keeping both religious views in play, Shakespeare could tease the audience with religious scenes that simultaneously inspire doubt, conviction, and confusion. Hamlet is wary of Horatio's ghost from the beginning (I.ii.) and knows the dead do not return from the grave.[142]

Scot takes things a step further, saying the apparition might be knavery. The ghost in *Hamlet* is neither

---

[140] Wright, "All Done with Mirrors," 179.

[141] Protestant views are expressed in Ludwig Lavater's *Of Ghosts and Spirits Walking in the Night*, published 1570-1596. Wilson writes, "Hamlet himself is clearly steeped in the opinion which Lavater expounds ..." (Wilson, *What Happens in "Hamlet,"* 63.)

[142] "Le Loyer quotes Chrysostom to the effect that when an apparition claims to be the spirit of a particular person, one should expect a deception of the devil." Pierre Le Loyer, *Livres des Spectres ou Apparitions et Vision d'Esprit, Anges et Demons*" (Angers 1586), bk. 3, chap. 7, quoted in Jenkins, *Arden Shakespeare "Hamlet,"* 483.

spirit nor demon and the conspirators against the murderous Claudius do not choose just any "ghost," but the ghost of Hamlet's father to convey the murder story. Why would these measures need to be taken to get the murder story into Hamlet's head? Costuming the ghost in full battle armor would virtually hide who wears it. A ghost, dressed as old Hamlet, in full battle armor like the king wore "when he the ambitious Norway combated" (I.i.), would have been a costume familiar at court and recognizable as old Hamlet to guards on dark, lonely guard platforms along castle walls. Sections or layers of castle walls would form barriers between the ghost and the observers. Even the ghost's stride and mannerisms would be masked as the pretender struts awkwardly about, armed head to toe in portentous form. This would also allow the director to lend some humor to the menacing character. That the ghost "assumes [Hamlet's] noble father's person" (I.ii.), helps convince a more curious than offended Hamlet to watch for the ghost to appear that night. The impersonator of a dead person tells the story so no one has to bear responsibility for knowing and sharing the murder story with Hamlet. The story can go unchallenged. Sources remain anonymous. This ghost has authority, cover, and leverage.

The hoax relies on disguise, superstition, Hamlet's disease, and his intense resentment of Claudius. Through the ages, the powerful have hidden behind deception and secret acts to promulgate falsehoods and coerce actions. Those weakened with illness, poverty, resentment, or ignorance are more easily deceived and abused. The motives and weaknesses may change, but the process of deception and coercion continues. As Elizabethan/post-medieval England began to seek more natural explanations for ghosts and superstitions, the ghost in *Hamlet* cautiously sides with Dee and Scot. The ghost invites Elizabethans and Jacobeans to view natural explanations for magic (illusion) and to question even the views of the new king, James I.

TRUE AVOUCH OF MINE OWN EYES

In Act 1, scene 4, Hamlet is understandably puzzled by the ghost's questionable shape and wants to know what is behind it. This puzzlement is trumped by the information bizarrely communicated to him that his Uncle Claudius murdered his father. In the tradition of theater ghosts, the ghost bemoans a tragic loss and demands revenge. But Hamlet, the modern hero and scholar, understands the ghost is a trick. The text tells us the ghost truly appears, but the ghost is a safely staged, cowardly, and indecipherable means to coerce him to commit regicide. Neither spirit nor hallucination (collective or personal), it appears to several people several times. This ghost appears twice to two guards, making two eyewitnesses at two separate events. It appears two more times to one of those guards. It appears three times to Horatio and twice to Hamlet. There is much to make us doubt the ghost is supernatural — it is intended to reveal trickery. Shakespeare confirms the modern era, redefining the theater ghost and creating in his Hamlet a new character dimension: the actor recognizes an illusion contrived by cowards to communicate a catastrophic demand.[143] Why would Shakespeare's Hamlet accept

---

[143] Scot, *Discoverie of Witchcraft*, Bk. 8, chap. 1, "[G]od will not give his ... power to a creature. ... St. Augustine ... proveth the ceasing of miracles: now blind flesh dooth not open the eies of the blind by the miracle of God but the eies of our hart are opened by the word of God. Now is

the manifestation as a ghost? Let us assume that Hamlet, whose sanity is most often in question, responds to the ghost sanely: he recognizes it is a hoax. He continues to respond sanely, while Horatio and the guards seem to have lost their sanity and view what appears as the ghost of Hamlet's father.

Studies focus on whether the ghost is good or evil; from heaven, hell, or purgatory; Protestant or Catholic; visible or imaginary. W. W. Greg writes, "No one will suggest that the apparition is pure fancy, but it is a long cry from that to the belief that it is supernatural," and says one could "explain it away as we should any other spook."[144] But Greg speculates the ghost may be "a freak of collective suggestion" and does not take his argument far enough.

Martin Scofield writes, "In sudden, nearly hysterical relief of his feelings Hamlet turns the ghost into a comic demon: 'Well said, old mole, canst work in the earth so fast?' A 'worthy pioneer', and 'ha boy, say'st thou

---

not our dead carcase raised ... by miracle, but our dead bodies be still in the grave, and our soules are raised to life by Christ."

[144] Greg, "Hamlet's Hallucination," 410. Greg goes on to say, "Further, it seems ... there is about the appearance something to confirm the belief that it is the dead King in a mind in which the suggestion is always present. But we do not know how the belief originally arose; whether from an actually convincing resemblance, or whether through the opportune congress of some chance phenomenon with the preoccupation in the minds of the officers, Marcellus and Bernardo. From the freedom of Hamlet's discourse in their presence, we may suppose them to have been loyal followers of his father; and the events of the last few weeks must have given rise to speculation and suspicion in the minds of others than the Prince. ... To many people, Horatio's evidence is conclusive regarding the genuineness of the Ghost. But on close examination we have found that, for all his honesty, he is a very bad witness indeed. From him, the suggestion passes to Hamlet. And we may fancy we trace how the idea, once formed, works in diverse ways upon the belief of each. There is the appearance of mutual suggestion; the characters encourage one another to trace the likeness of the King."

so? Art thou there truepenny? Come on. You hear this fellow in the cellarage.'"[145] Scofield writes that Hamlet makes the ghost into something comic as a relief. But the ghost charade is indeed something comic, and Hamlet's lines show that he knows this. He may also be hoping to coax Horatio, the Wittenberg scholar, out of his puzzling belief in the ghost. When this does not happen, Hamlet begins to realize there is an assassin at court who will not stop at killing a king or Hamlet himself, and this assassin is his despised uncle, his mother's husband. The ghost may be awkwardly comical at times, but its revelation is not.

The ghost's story cannot be corroborated and isn't even original—it is a play already known to Hamlet (and Horatio?).[146] For months, the ghost does not bother to appear again. As Hamlet tries to decide what to do, it matters less to him how the story of the murder was communicated. He cannot rely on the statement of a ghost to prove Claudius's guilt, nor can he summon a ghost for further questioning. For him, the larger problem becomes what the ghost has communicated, not the ghost itself.

The ghost's shenanigans call to mind a narrative in Scot's *Discoverie of Witchcraft*. When the wife of the mayor of Orleans, France, died (around 1534), it was learned that she had earlier requested a simple funeral and burial in the church of the Franciscans. The mayor's meager financial support insulted the monks, and they vowed to damn the wife's soul forever. Two doctors of divinity devised a scheme whereby one

---

[145] Scofield, *The Ghosts of Hamlet*, 120.

[146] Greg writes, "Not only has he presumably seen it [*The Murder of Gonzago*] acted at Wittenberg, but he knows the original Italian play or novel on which it was founded," in "Hamlet's Hallucination," 415.

of the novices was placed above the church's arches and directed to make loud rumblings at the midnight prayers. The priest would then question this "spirit." Eventually, communicating its answers through counted strikes on a board, the spirit identified itself as the mayor's wife. Leaders of the community were present when the counterfeit spirit revealed that it was a damned spirit, damned through Luther's heresy. The monks demanded the wife's body be removed from the church and asked the citizens to back them. The citizens refused. A bishop came to investigate the matter, but one of the doctors of divinity stiffly refused to cooperate. The mayor brought the matter before the king whose court held an inquiry in Paris. Given promises of protection from punishment and from the monks, the novice playing the counterfeit ghost confessed to the hoax. The monks were sent back to Orleans and cast into prison. This story, from Scot's *Discoverie of Witchcraft*, resonates with the scheme attempted against Hamlet.[147]

Deepening Shakespeare's play, and adding to Hamlet's dilemmas, would be the already mentioned either/or pronouncement about ghosts from *The Discoverie of Witchcraft*. We recall that the author, a Christian, denied the possibility of spirits assuming material form, claiming that such would either be the illusion of a melancholic mind or flat knavery on the part of some rogue.[148] Flat knavery performed as an illusion against someone of a melancholic mind would yield stronger effects, both because the victim is an easier target and because his understanding of the illusion might not be taken seriously. Having seen

---

[147] Scot, *Discoverie of Witchcraft*, Bk. 15, chap. 23.

[148] Wilson, *What Happens in "Hamlet,"* 64, and Scot, *Discoverie of Witchcraft*.

an apparition in material form, Hamlet's weakened though educated reasoning is given another challenge: is he that crazy (illusions produced in the melancholic mind), or is someone playing tricks on him (flat knavery on the part of some rogue)?

> The spirit that I have seen
> May be a devil, and the devil hath power
> T'assume a pleasing shape. Yea, and perhaps
> Out of my weakness and my melancholy,
> As he is very potent with such spirits,
> Abuses me to damn me! (II.ii. 533-538)

Hamlet suffers from melancholy and is emotionally strained, but he is not ignorant. He and spectators know that the apparition has appeared not only to him but also to others and on more than one occasion. This limits the choice to "flat knavery on the part of some rogue."

Staging this knavery to fit what is spoken in the text has challenged directors.[149] Eleanor Prosser writes that critics have agreed the ghost "is not a mere folk ghost: a graveyard spook ... not a mere pagan ghost: a forlorn soul seeking proper burial ... The nature of the Ghost is thrown into question as it is in no other play of the Elizabethan or Jacobean period ..."[150] E. Pearlman offers this assessment: "The Ghost of Hamlet is no less of this world than any other character in the play, and yet he is set apart because his every word and gesture challenges the deeply-held conviction that by rights he ought to be different. Shakespeare's reimagining of the Ghost is a triumph of art that is all the more impressive for its neat

---

[149] For example, "It shrunk in haste away and vanished." Act 1, scene 2, 218-219.

[150] Prosser, *Hamlet and Revenge*, 101.

invisibility."[151] David Brailow writes that the ghost in *Hamlet* presents multiple problems and opportunities for directors.[152] Although the texts contain few stage directions for the ghost, spoken lines indicate how it appears and disappears. With multiple appearances to multiple people, already spectators know this is no "freak of collective suggestion" and no ordinary ghost — theatrical or otherwise.[153] It is first described as an apparition, something remarkable, appearing with a fearsome, frowning, warlike demeanor, and in the very armor old Hamlet wore when he fought Norway. Later, the ghost is described as having his beaver up, a pale countenance of sorrow, sable silvered beard, and eyes fixed constantly upon them. Then, after appearing to Horatio in company of the two guards, it appears to be offended and, despite Horatio's protests, stalks away without speaking.

In *Rescripting Shakespeare*, theater historian Alan Dessen offers that there may have been a stage convention available at the Globe for presenting vanishing and the supernatural.[154] Understanding the structure of the Elizabethan stage helps the director visualize possibilities for matching action and plot to

---

[151]   E. Pearlman, "Shakespeare at Work: The Invention of the Ghost," in *"Hamlet": New Critical Essays*, ed. Arthur F. Kinney (New York: Routledge, 2002), 80-81.

[152]   David Brailow, "'Tis heere. 'Tis gone.' The Ghost in the Text," in *Stage Directions in "Hamlet,"* ed. Aasand, 101-114.

[153]   "H. A. Mason has written on the suspicious and contradictory character of the Ghost in the first act: for him there's no doubt it is something fishy. The words used to describe the Ghost — 'thing, 'dreaded sight', 'apparition', 'illusion', 'like the king' and 'in the same figure like the king that's dead' — all suggest doubt about what the Ghost actually is." Scofield, *The Ghosts of Hamlet*, 140. And see H. A. Mason, "The Ghost in 'Hamlet,' A Resurrected 'Paper,'" *Cambridge Quarterly* 3, no. 2 (1967-8): 127-152.

[154]   Dessen, *Rescripting Shakespeare*, 148.

characters' lines. In opening scenes, the ghost's actor is at times located in the cellarage (the "hell"), an area under the stage platform about five feet high.[155] This area could use curtains to conceal or reveal below-stage action. A trapdoor would open up to this space, and the ghost's lines could be spoken from here, perhaps using a pipe-like device to project its voice while the ghost player or projected image would appear onstage.[156] [157] This speaker of the ghost's lines in the theater hell could be seen by (some) spectators if the curtain surrounding this area were pulled back. This is the understanding of Hamlet's back and forth jabs and jokes about the "old

---

[155] Colin Butler's *The Practical Shakespeare: The Plays in Practice and on the Page* (Athens: Ohio University Press, 2005), contains helpful illustrations and descriptions of the Elizabethan stage. Also see McDonald's *Bedford Companion to Shakespeare*, 47. Stages at Hampton Court had raised platforms. Also see John H. Astington's *English Court Theatre 1558-1642* (Cambridge: Cambridge University Press, 1999), 211.

[156] Porta was an Italian dramatist. In *Natural Magick*, "Giambattista della Porta also writes of the transmission of sound through pipes in 1589. ... '[I]f any man shall make leaden Pipes exceeding long, two or three hundred paces long ... and shall speak in them some or many words, they will be carried true through those Pipes, and be heard at the other end, as they came from the speakers mouth.'" Philip Butterworth, *Magic on the Early English Stage* (Cambridge: Cambridge University Press, 2005), 105. And see the translation of (John Baptista) Porta's *Natural Magick* (London: for Thomas Young & Samuel Speed, 1658), Bk. 19, chap.1.

[157] A story is told that when William Cecil was a young law student, a companion enticed him to play at gambling. Cecil lost all his money, bedding and books to the companion. Later, among other friends, he said the companion had misled him and he would get even. "With a long tronke [pipe], he made a hole in the wall, nere his plaie-fellow's bede-head and in a fearfull voice, spake thus thorough the tronke. 'O mortall man, repent! Repent of thy ... time [in] plaie ... or els thou art damned ...'" The man was very frightened and the next day told the youths how a fearful voice had spoken to him. He vowed never to gamble again. He asked Cecil to forgive him and restored all of Cecil's things. See Edward Nares, *Memoirs of the Life and Administration of the Right Honourable William Cecil, Lord Burghley, ...* vol. 1 (London: Saunders and Otley, 1828), 59

mole," as Hamlet creates a bond of understanding with spectators, knowing what some of them can see.[158] This would also have been an appealing and relatively new set of what we would now call special effects, a new level of viewing, enjoying, and understanding theater.

Remember that in Shakespeare's time, the actor-manager would have had the master copy for which he could create stage directions. Sedition, religion, and conjuring were among topics censored from plays.[159] What had been written into the text would have to get past the Office of Revels, the royal censor. But stage directions left blank for the director's imagination, daring, and circumstance could escape censorship.[160] After the court's reprimand for performing *Richard II* and the shock, if not grief, at the swift trial and beheading of the Earl of Essex, Shakespeare may have wanted overt and covert changes to his *Hamlet*. Shakespeare had the necessary skills and imagination

---

[158] "Historical critics (E. E. Stoll, J. Dover Wilson, and particularly Eleanor Prosser) have shown that Elizabethan audiences would have responded to the ghost in a generally suspicious way." Scofield, *The Ghosts of Hamlet*, 139.

[159] "The publishing history of Shakespeare's plays at this time (1598-99) suggests that it was wiser for the Chamberlain's Men to publish lightly sanitized versions and pull offending plays from the repertory, rather than let linger the memory of what might otherwise be regarded as seditious history." Shapiro, *A Year in the Life of William Shakespeare*, 137.

[160] Edmund Tilney, who led the Office of Revels 1579-1610, was the "longest serving Master, presiding over a period of central importance in English theatrical and dramatic history." Astington, *English Court Theatre*, 20.
"[A] commission of 1581 … gave [the Master of Revels] authority 'to order and reforme, autorise and put downe' all plays, players, and playing spaces throughout the realm as he saw fit. All theatrical licensing, in theory, was therefore now in the hands of the crown, and the commission announced to actors and to local authorities alike that their interests could be pursued only with royal assent." Astington, *English Court Theatre*, 22.

to align certain themes of the play with troubled times; he shakes playgoers out of scientifically or politically indefensible positions, while reclothing the players in the intrigues and mortal betrayals of the time.

Suppose Q1, found in 1823, is a pirated incomplete text of a less censored version of Shakespeare's *Hamlet*. A difference between Q1 (1603, sometimes referred to as a pirated copy) and Q2 (1604) is that Q1 calls things directly by name, while Q2 handles everything more discreetly and with more sophistication, leaving less obvious the actors' intentions.[161] Court censors may have wanted to cut the Q1 scene where Horatio and the queen discuss the king's treachery (roughly following Q2's IV.v.); or Hamlet's charges against King Claudius just before Osric enters to tell them of the proposed duel (V.ii.); or when he asks Horatio if it isn't with perfect conscience that he can pay the king back by killing him and asks further if it is not to be damned to let the king, "this canker of our nature," live to create more evil (V.ii.); or the entrance of Voltemand (Voltemar) in the final scene (V.ii). If Q1, after 1909 generally referred to as the "bad quarto," was an attempt to get off a quick printing of Shakespeare's play before King James could forbid, censor, or burn it, it may be closest to Shakespeare's hand. The actor William Poel staged the Q1 text (in 1881) in Elizabethan costumes, believing that Q1 "represents more truly [Shakespeare's] dramatic conception than either Quarto 2 or our stage version."[162]

---

[161] "[D]er Unterschied der beiden Quartos ist hier, wie ueberall, dass die Q1 die Dinge direkt beim Namen nennt, die Q2 alles feiner, diskreter behandelt, und die Intentionen der Handelnden mehr verschleiert." From Hendrik De Groot, *"Hamlet," Its Textual History* (Amsterdam: Swets & Zeitlinger, 1923), 49.

[162] Hubler and Barnet, *Tragedy of Hamlet, Prince of Denmark*, 282.

Dialogue provides the essential guide to stage directions. Alan Dessen advises, "Given the dearth of stage directions in the printed texts of the period, the would-be reconstructer of Elizabethan-Jacobean onstage procedures often must build upon the evidence in the dialogue, a seemingly logical avenue to pursue but one fraught with difficulties."[163] With the authority granted the director over the earliest surviving texts, directors of *Hamlet* benefit by carefully considering the motivations behind the spoken words. "[I]t seems to me," writes Scofield, "that some such imaginative latitude must be allowed the reader or audience if they are to make sense of the play at all. We must often infer what has happened in the plot of a play from what is implied but not stated."[164] What could be seen did not have to be printed as stage directions. After 1599, Shakespeare refers to playgoers as spectators.[165] The story is carried as much by what is seen as by what is heard, and actions imbedded in dialogue become richer because they drive stage directions. Wilson also made the case for stage directions derived from the spoken lines, when he puts Hamlet within range of hearing that Claudius and Polonius will spy on him and Ophelia.[166] Stage directions based on spoken lines would follow a director's understanding of the spectators' needs (such as empathy for the characters and continuity of plot and action) and give the production the various degrees of impact the director desires and the play deserves.

---

163   Alan Dessen, *Recovering Shakespeare's Theatrical Vocabulary* (Cambridge: Cambridge University Press, 1995), 200.

164   Scofield, *The Ghosts of Hamlet*, 161.

165   Shapiro, *A Year in the Life of William Shakespeare*, 29.

166   Wilson, *What Happens in "Hamlet,"* 108.

Shakespeare surely varied his script and stage directions depending on the audience, year, stage, theater house, political risks, and availability of actors and props. Plays were performed at public playhouses and at court. There were indoor and outdoor public (pay to attend) playhouses. Orgel describes how the cost of admission stratified playgoers into an economic hierarchy — a penny to stand, two pennies to sit, three for front row seats, and a shilling for a gentleman's or lord's private box.[167]

Plays for the monarch and other royalty functioned differently. These plays took place at court or at a private estate or university. In these performances, the monarch was part of the show, and the director would know where the monarch and other royalty would be seated. Once the king's or queen's seat was established, Orgel writes, "the audience around him at once became a living emblem of the structure of the court. The closer one sat to the monarch the 'better' one's place was, an index to one's status ..."[168]

Court, university, and private performances were usually indoors, where, with daylight excluded, a director would have more control over lighting effects. Dessen asks if the ghost's exits "require something trickier, more illusionistic?"[169] I believe Iain Wright would answer as he has written: by "Dee and Shakespeare's time there was ... an extensive literature on how to float artificial spectres in midair with the aid of concave mirrors and the technology was advancing

[167] Stephen Orgel, *The Illusion of Power: Political Theater in the English Renaissance* (Los Angeles: UC Berkeley Press, 1975), 8.

[168] Orgel, *The Illusion of Power*, 11.

[169] Dessen, *Recovering Shakespeare's Theatrical Vocabulary*, 200.

rapidly."[170] When Shakespeare staged the ghost scenes in *Hamlet*, he could double the dramatic and the political impact by daring to use "magic" (light, shadow, projection, reflection) to project the image of the ghost, thus cutting the edge of Elizabethan consciousness between what medieval sentiment would take to be supernatural/demonic apparitions and what the more learned would know were optical illusions.[171]
Scot writes:

> [The] woonderous devises, and miraculous sights and conceipts made and conteined in glasse, doo fare exceed all other; whereto the art perspective is verie necessarie. For it sheweth the illusions of them, whose experiments be seene in diverse sorts of glasses; ... Others are so framed ... wherby you shall see men hanging in the aire; ... others, wherin you may see one comming, & another going; ... others that represent not the images received within them, but cast them farre off in the aire, appearing like aierie images ...[172]

In "Come like shadowes, so depart," Wright argues that Shakespeare used special lighting effects in indoor settings to create the illusion of ghostly kings.[173] These ideas, when applied to the staging of the ghost in *Hamlet*,

---

170 Wright continues, "The great breakthrough had come with the invention of the silvered glass mirror by the Venetians at the beginning of the sixteenth century. ... Now startlingly life-like images were possible." "All Done with Mirrors," 188.

171 Scot offers a defense for conjurors who use illusion and practices of confederacie and legierdemaine: "[W]hen these experiments growe to superstition or impietie, they are either to be forsaken as vaine, or denied as false. Howbeit, if these things be done for mirth and recreation, and not to hurt of our neighbour, nor to the abusing or prophaning of Gods name, in mine opinion, they are neither impious nor altogether unlawfull: though a naturall thing be made to seeme supernaturall." *Discoverie of Witchcraft*, bk. 13, chap. 12.

172 Scot, *Discoverie of Witchcraft*, bk. 13, chap. 19.

173 Iain Wright, "'Come like shadowes, so depart': The Ghostly Kings in *Macbeth*," *The Shakespearean International Yearbook* 6 (Oct. 2006), 215-229.

would lend support to the ghost's being played as an attempt to coerce someone through illusion. Pointing to John Dee, Roger Bacon, and Reginald Scot, Wright believes there is plenty of evidence for the use of such theatrical technique in the later sixteenth century.

Centuries before Shakespeare, the thirteenth century's "founder of modern science," Roger Bacon, had described how to use concave mirrors to produce apparitions in order to terrify enemies of the realm. As early as the 1400s, polished bowls served as mirrors to reflect light and could be moved to create an early spotlight.[174] A book from John Dee's library (*Three Books of Occult Philosophy*, 1531) reported Aristotle's claim that "'by the artificialness of certain looking-glasses, may be produced at a distance in the Air, beside the looking-glass what images we please; which when ignorant men see, they think they see the appearances of spirits, or souls, when indeed, they are nothing else but semblances kin to themselves, and without life.'"

Giambattista della Porta's *Magia Naturalis* (1558-1559, 1589) was a hit long before *Hamlet* was printed. Porta, a scholar and playwright, describes a *camera obscura* where "we may see in a chamber things that are not." Even without sunlight, "you may see in the dark what is light without by reason of Torches. [With] Torches or lights ... in Chambers, we may see in another dark Chamber what is done ... [At] night the image of anything may be seen hanging in the middle of the Chamber, that will terrify the beholders. Fit the Image before the hole that you desire to make to seem hanging in the Air in another chamber that is dark; let there be many Torches ... In the middle of the dark Chamber, place a white sheet, or some solid thing that may receive the Image sent in: for the spectators that

---

[174] Butterworth, *Magic on the Early English Stage*, 80-81.

see not the sheet will see the image hanging in the Air, very clear ..." (See the 1658 English translation, *Natural Magick*, bk. 17, chap. 6-7, 12).

The play's ghost has the quality of an invulnerable cloudy shape; it can fade, shrink, and vanish. These actions require something more than the typical entrance and exit. What the characters in *Hamlet* say about the ghost anticipates the use of a reflection or mirrored projection. The apparition "appears ... with solemn march ... and very pale ... it shrunk in haste away and vanished from our sight." The ghost evades the strikes of the partisan: "Tis here. ... Tis here. ... Tis gone." "It is as the air, invulnerable, and our vain blows malicious mockery"; and later, "it faded." Such descriptions could be staged through, in Dessen's words, "theatrical technology or trickery."[175] Skillful use of a projected image for the ghost could provide a fitting and entertaining solution for matching action to what the characters say.

Strong illumination was a desired effect in Elizabethan plays, and every effort was made to produce intense dispersed illumination and create an inspired atmosphere.[176] Wright describes a magic lantern device, a design he located in a Venetian manuscript from the fifteenth century.[177] With this device, the ghost of King Hamlet could be projected from the cellarage or an adjoining room onto a surface onstage, perhaps through a window or portal, or battlement.[178]

With the proper staging conditions, Shakespeare would have enjoyed using projection techniques for

---

[175] Dessen, *Recovering Shakespeare's Theatrical Vocabulary*, 198.

[176] Astington, *English Court Theatre*, 96.

[177] Wright, "'Come like shadowes, so depart,'" 222.

[178] Part of the Elizabethan stage was the "empty space," typically behind a curtain between the two doors on either side of the stage.

the ghost, not only for the actors, but also for what the spectators — perhaps selected spectators — would or would not have been able to see. The ghost in the queen's closet (III.iv.) could appear as projected behind the portal, a deep opening, leaving the interesting effect that Hamlet sees the ghost, but the queen does not. Some in the theater will see it, and some will not. This would lead to lively, perhaps even uncomfortable after-theater conversations. Staging the ghost as an illusion that instigates much evil is what Shakespeare, in those perilous and changing times, would have preferred.

Shakespeare's acting company played before Queen Elizabeth each of her last nine years. The queen died in March 1603, and that summer, James VI of Scotland succeeded her to become James I of England. He renamed the company "The King's Men," and they continued to perform at court. Within a year of the queen's death, a version of Shakespeare's *Hamlet* (Q1) appeared in print.

Wright suggests that in the summer of 1603, when Shakespeare's acting company was staying at Mortlake, Shakespeare and John Dee were meeting.[179] "If Dee and Shakespeare were not already acquainted, I find it hard to believe that they would not have become so on this occasion."[180] John Dee would have eagerly coached Shakespeare in staging techniques to artificially float a ghost (demon?) in front of Dee's powerful critic and self-proclaimed authority on demons: King James. Orgel describes a theater technique used after 1605 and "*only* at court or when royalty was present — the monarch became the center of theatrical experience in another way ... In a theater employing perspective,

---

[179] Queen Elizabeth, Lord Burghley, and Walsingham had all visited John Dee at Mortlake with strong interest in Dee's knowledge and skills.

[180] Wright, "All Done with Mirrors," 183.

there is only one focal point, one perfect place in the hall from which the illusion achieves its fullest effect. ... [T]his is where the king sat."[181] Wright reasons that to put magic on stage in the sixteenth and seventeenth centuries exposes it: "if actors can plausibly fabricate it, night after night, how much other supposed magic may be produced by the same means?"[182] This puts the lie to using illusion as a way to control or persecute people.[183] A dramatic purpose of *Hamlet* may have been to convert the conscience of the monarch.

As Wilson reminds us, some in post medieval England, despite a veneer of Protestantism, still believed in spirits of the departed; ghost scenes in *Hamlet* "came upon [them] with all the force of a fresh and unexpected revelation of the spirit world."[184] Shakespeare's fresh and unexpected revelation of the spirit world was that the spirit world could be artificially produced to deceive and then reproduced onstage using illusion, the magicians' stock and trade.

This emerging and enticing understanding of the mechanics of illusion threads another band of tension among the existing strands of Catholicism,

---

[181] Orgel, *The Illusion of Power*, 10.

[182] Wright, "All Done with Mirrors," 199.

[183] Sir David Brewster describes ways in which the ancients used illusion and states that these "operations of the ancient magic, though sufficiently indicative of the methods which were employed, are too meager to convey any idea of the splendid and imposing exhibitions which must have been displayed. A national system of deception, intended as an instrument of government, must have brought into requisition not merely the scientific skill of the age, but a variety of subsidiary contrivances, calculated to astonish the beholder, to confound his judgment, to dazzle his senses, and to give a predominant influence to the peculiar imposture which it was thought desirable to establish." Brewster, *Letters on Natural Magic Addressed to Sir Walter Scott* (London: John Murray, 1832), 68.

[184] Wilson, *What Happens in "Hamlet,"* 58.

Protestantism, witchcraft, and science. To transition spectators away from medieval mindscapes and create additional layers of meaning, I believe Shakespeare experimented with techniques of illusion. I also believe Shakespeare's *Hamlet* is too rich to be impoverished by the lack of such techniques.[185] The ghost can be played as "flat knavery" regardless of form — optical illusion, or onstage actor.

---

[185] "[I]t is surely arguable that part of the fascination of this play is precisely its refusal to give us all the answers and its resistance to yield to any 'theory.'" Thompson and Taylor, *Arden Shakespeare "Hamlet,"* 135.

CHAPTER FOUR:

THE PLAY'S THE THING

This book's understanding of *Hamlet* requires a shift away from the popular post-1660s views of Horatio, the ghost, and Fortinbras, but it does not affect all the play's themes. Debate will continue about whether Hamlet hesitates too long. The queen's guilt or innocence, Claudius's motives, King Hamlet's character, Ophelia's madness, and the deaths of Rosencrantz and Guildenstern are just a few themes not specifically addressed here.

Hamlet is a play, not a novel. Action, gesture, tone, speech, and spectacle carry the story. My interpretation takes nothing from the play and adds depth and integrity. In this more complex view, spoken lines do not change and are enriched with more verve, humor, poignancy, context, and follow-through. In creating stage directions, the director can "by indirections find directions out" (II.i.). He or she creates the play as an artist creates a painting utilizing empty spaces to unify forms. In the last scene of the play, playgoers learn that Horatio writes the "official" version of *The Tragedy of Hamlet*. But sideshows, played out beneath the stage, on side stages, in the "discovery space," from the gallery, and on outer or inner stage areas, reveal collusions, deceptions, and "accidental judgments."

This chapter suggests staging for scenes most relevant to my interpretation. Please refer to the book's preface for text sources and see McDonald's helpful descriptions of Elizabethan stages on pages 45-51 in *The Bedford Companion to Shakespeare*. In staging this long play, the director needs to give priority to characters unique to Shakespeare's *Hamlet* and to actions repeated in each of the earliest texts. David Ball, in his manual for directors, advises, "If you trust the play enough to stage it, trust its author."[186] He refers specifically to the lines between Polonius and Reynaldo (II.i) and advises that cutting or altering these might change how we understand a central character's actions. Voltemand, Cornelius, Fortinbras (except his entrance in the last scene), Polonius's advice to Laertes, Hamlet's advice to the players, and Hamlet's soliloquy ("How all things do inform against me.") were regrettably cut from the late 1600s Betterton text.[187] Changes, some more drastic, continued into the 1700s; David Garrick rewrites Act 5. By the 1800s, some cut Fortinbras entirely and focus more on the love between Hamlet and Ophelia.

Another priority is to leave the play in the appropriate time setting. Alan Dessen describes some problems that result from moving a Shakespeare play to a later time period — especially "when scripted signals for weaponry jar with a reconfiguration to a later period."[188] Dessen offers several examples including *Henry IV Pt. 1*, Act 5, scene 4. Here, if actors wore modern military dress instead of knightly armor, it would "diminish Shakespeare's

---

[186] David Ball, *Backwards and Forwards*, 83.

[187] Edward Hubler and Sylvan Barnet, eds., *Tragedy of Hamlet, Prince of Denmark* by William Shakespeare (New York: Signet Classics, Penguin, 1987), 277.

[188] Dessen, *Rescripting Shakespeare*, 136.

emphasis upon counterfeit kings" who dress like kings.[189] Taken out of the 1475-1540 time limits, *Hamlet* loses the effect of outdated full body armor worn as a disguise; this would also lose the loaded reference to Wittenberg, a seedbed for the Reformation.

Changes in time setting, drastic text alterations, and the elimination of characters unique to Shakespeare's *Hamlet* persist because we neglect to seek Shakespeare's intentions. Casting Horatio as accomplice to Fortinbras requires adjusting the delivery of his lines, to make Horatio's disposition one of control and intrigue, while still projecting a degree of loyalty to Hamlet. After all, Hamlet would probably view the enemy of his father's murderer as his friend. Once Horatio has signed on to the business of murder, more bodies fall than was his purpose. My preference would leave enough softness in Horatio's character to imply that he wants Hamlet to live to be a figurehead royal, where Horatio would share actual control with Fortinbras.[190] At play's end, Fortinbras is aware of this intended compromise to his own crown: "Let four captains bear Hamlet like a soldier to the stage, for he was likely, had he been put on, to have proved most royal."

Act 1, scene 1

The play opens with action to set up the opening line, "Who's there?" spoken by the sentry, Barnardo.[191] Voltemand and Francisco stand watch, while behind

---

[189] Dessen, *Rescripting Shakespeare*, 138.

[190] If Hamlet hadn't been poisoned, perhaps he and Fortinbras would have dueled for control in the last scene, fairly reenacting their dead fathers' duel.

[191] Alan Dessen describes how "a lengthy pre-show sequence [for *All's Well That Ends Well*] started with a seated Lavatch and two children (younger

them in the discovery space, Horatio helps Osric into cap-a-pie armor.[192] Francisco and Osric both have access to armor. The playhouses used elaborate costumes and Osric's armor is probably authentic.[193] Norman and Pottinger illustrate how a servant would help a knight put on armor.[194] Horatio has his back to the spectators, but there is about him some marker or trait that at a later point will identify him as Osric's helper. This lag in identifying Horatio holds the spectators' curiosity and gives them needed room to doubt that he is part of the trickery. Acceptance of this intrigue comes reluctantly. Seen this way, the play has more (albeit dark) comic scenes, as the collaborators try to get the armored Osric to do things. Osric puts the helmet on, and Horatio nods approvingly.

versions of Bertram and Helena) who disappeared to be replaced by their adult counterparts." Dessen, *Rescripting Shakespeare*, 79.

[192] The discovery space is an area to the rear of the stage, which can be covered or closed. A scrim covering could be used. With proper lighting, the scrim could conceal or reveal characters and actions.

[193] Stephen Orgel quotes a 1599 theater visitor, "'the comedians are very expensively and elegantly costumed, since it is usual in England, when important gentlemen or knights die, for their finest clothes to be bequeathed to their servants, and since it is not proper for them to wear such clothes, instead they subsequently give them to the comedians to purchase very cheaply.'" Orgel, *The Illusion of Power*, 5.

[194] A. V. B. Norman and Don Pottinger, *A History of War and Weapons, 449-1660*, (New York: Thomas Y. Crowell and Company, 1966), 118-120.

Figure 7. [195]

While Francisco stands watch for them, Horatio and Voltemand use a pulley or winch (windlass) to hoist Osric up to the platform from which he will later appear.[196] "Elizabethan playhouses had a certain amount of machinery — trapdoors in the stage and in the roof above the stage, winches for descents of deities ..."[197] Francisco then reoccupies his guard position, and Voltemand remains hidden where he can lower Osric from the platform.[198] Barnardo will soon be relieving Francisco, so Horatio rushes off, but in his haste he accidentally makes noise. The noise frightens the approaching Barnardo and prompts his "Who's

---

[195] Charles Knight, ed., *The Pictorial Edition of the Works of Shakspere, Tragedies,* vol. 1 (London: C. Knight & Co., 1843), 101. Courtesy of Special Collections, Kenneth Spencer Research Library, University of Kansas Libraries.

[196] And see Butterworth, *Magic on the Early English Stage,* 175.

[197] Orgel, *The Illusion of Power,* 5.

[198] If one opts for the more fitting projection of the ghost as illusion, Voltemand may be seen testing the projection of the armored Osric.

there?" As Jan Blits points out, this is "an inversion of normal military order, the question is asked by the relieving sentinel [Barnardo] and not the one on duty [Francisco]."[199]

A jittery Francisco admits to Barnardo that although he's had a quiet watch with "not a mouse stirring," he is sick at heart. When he asks who is approaching them, Horatio identifies himself with Marcellus as "friends to this ground." Marcellus adds that they are also loyal subjects of the King of Denmark. After his "Give you goodnight," Francisco leaves his post, and out of the other players' view, he joins Voltemand to help manage the ghost.

Imagine the ghost scenes at the guard platform as a play within a play where Horatio serves as both director and lead actor. When Barnardo asks if it is Horatio with Marcellus, Horatio replies that it is "a piece of him." Horatio has already made the ghost appear to Marcellus and Barnardo, with whom he apparently keeps company. Horatio knows that the guards will speak to him about the ghost as he is a scholar, and the common belief was that ghosts would speak to scholars. Horatio has mocked them in their belief that they have seen a ghost and so accompanies Marcellus to see if the ghost will appear again. He knows it will because he has set up the ghost's appearances. He plays the skeptic so that when the ghost appears, his won-over belief is that much more convincing. Horatio needs the guards' backing as witnesses because it will not be easy to convince Hamlet, the Wittenberg student, that the armored appearance is a ghost.

While on watch, Marcellus begins to tell Horatio of the ghost's previous appearances. Then, from a

---

[199] Blits, *Deadly Thought*, 23.

platform not easily accessible to them, it appears again, and Barnardo calls it correctly— "in the same figure *like* the king that's dead" [my emphasis]. It is not the dead king but a figure dressed *like* him. The ghost is dressed in armor like old Hamlet used in battle, and Horatio knows how old Hamlet appeared in battle. Horatio instructs the guards that the ghost is as much like the (former) king as one is to oneself and that the armor is like the armor the old king wore in battle against Norway. Through statues, tapestries and other commemorations this kingly warlike pose may have been an appearance known to many. Put on the helmet and the beard, be stiff and ashen, maintain some distance, and the "questionable shape" becomes the ghost of old Hamlet.

Marcellus says, "Thou art a scholar, Horatio, speak to it." Pretending to be harrowed with fear, Horatio asks the ghost who he is that comes at this time of night, dressed in the warlike form of the buried king. It is convincing to the guards that someone as educated and knowledgeable as Horatio, stops scoffing and (acts like he) believes it is a ghost. Note that Horatio works not only to validate the appearance as a ghost, but also to clarify for them who they are seeing in the ghost. Horatio emphasizes to the guards that the ghost is real, not just a fancy, and he would not have believed it if he had not seen it with his own eyes. Horatio even claims that the ghost's frown is the same frown the dead king had shown in battle. He convinces them that it is the ghost of the dead Hamlet and accurately predicts that this ghost "bodes some strange eruption to our state." The confrontation achieves its objective. The ghost exits while Horatio orders it to stay and speak.

Horatio's prediction of a strange eruption to the state reminds Marcellus of the increased guard duty and other preparations for defense that seem to go on around the clock. He asks if anyone knows what this is about. At this, Horatio launches into his longest speech in the play and reveals a broad knowledge of the warring history and intrigue between Norway and Denmark. This long-winded speech from the later "yes-my-Lord" and "quite-so-my-Lord" Horatio has the attention of the play's opening scene and explains the motives and actions of Shakespeare's powerful, though seldom heard, Fortinbras. Horatio's knowledge of Fortinbras cannot be taken from center stage; clearly Horatio knows a great deal about him and the nature of his politics. In single combat, old Fortinbras lost his life and his lands to old Hamlet. Young Fortinbras seeks to regain "those foresaid lands so by his father lost." Not only has Horatio convinced the guards that the ghostly figure is a ghost, but Barnardo now adds that after hearing Horatio's explanation of the war preparations, he finds it especially fitting that the ghost of the warlike king would appear.

> Well may it sort that this portentous figure
> Comes armed through our watch so like the King
> That was and is the question of these wars.

This inspires Horatio to further tease the guards with another oration, this time about something the Roman Horatius (Horace) would have known well—the fall of Julius Caesar. Graves stood tenantless just before he fell, too. The ghost breaks Horatio off with another appearance. This could be the mechanically rigged appearance afforded by hoisting the ghost into view, but the descriptions of the ghost given by the guards would favor a reflected, projected, or mirrored image. This would create the illusion of the ghost and if used, it truly is illusion. Encouraged by how well things have gone so far, Horatio offers bold opposition to it, saying, "I'll cross it though it blast me," and "Stay, illusion!" Five times, he charges the ghost to speak to him, to tell them if he knows anything about Denmark's fate which they "happily foreknowing might avoid." The ghost does not speak to them.

Spoken lines describe the ghost as able to quickly shift positions and even disappear. Marcellus's partisan seems useless against it, "it is as the air, invulnerable, and our vain blows malicious mockery." When the ghost exits, Marcellus says it faded. Later, Horatio describes its exit: "it shrunk in haste away and vanished from our sight" (I.ii.). Horatio has a ready explanation for the ghost disappearing at first light, but the crowing of the cock would also signal daylight and risk exposing the "ghost." When Horatio says that the ghost "started, like a guilty thing upon a fearful summons," this could be comic with someone at side stage (Voltemand?), silently but dramatically letting the ghost know it's time to exit.

Horatio continues to direct the guards' understanding of this play within a play. He has given credence to the ghost, interpretation to its meaning, and now sets up the scene designed to lure young Hamlet into murdering Claudius. With the stage prepared to have Hamlet join them, Horatio accurately predicts that the ghost, though dumb to them, will speak to Hamlet. Horatio advises that in both love and duty, they need to tell Hamlet what they have seen:

Let us import what we have seen tonight
Unto young Hamlet, for upon my life
This spirit, dumb to us, will speak to him.
Do you consent we shall acquaint him with it,
As needful in our loves, fitting our duty?

Marcellus agrees and announces where they can meet him that same morning.

Horatio has sold the guards on the ghost and the trap is set. He has loaded the bait (the ghost) and set the spring (the meeting). He uses the guards to reduce the chance that Hamlet might not approach the trap. Now, spectators wait to see if the trap works on this Hamlet character and what the consequences will be.

Horatio, self-proclaimed "friend to this ground," controls the opening ghost scenes:

1. Having staged the ghost's appearances to the guards twice already, he convinces them that he wouldn't have believed there was a ghost if he hadn't seen it with his own eyes.
2. He identifies the apparition as the dead King Hamlet to tell them what they see.
3. He serves as the knowledgeable resource about ghosts and war preparations.
4. He bosses the ghost around (gives him stage directions).
5. He proposes the crucial and decisive meeting of Hamlet with the ghost.
6. He accurately predicts the strange eruption in their state, and that "this spirit, dumb to us, will speak to [Hamlet]."

Act I, scene 2

The urgency of the state of affairs between Norway
(as instigated by young Fortinbras) and Denmark is
repeated in King Claudius's warnings before Gertrude,
Polonius, Laertes, Hamlet, Voltemand, Cornelius, "cum
aliis [alijs]" (with others, including Osric). He informs
them that young Fortinbras, thinking Denmark is
weakened by the death of old Hamlet, is asking for the
surrender of those lands lost by his father to old Hamlet,
the recently deceased King of Denmark. This friction
between Norway and Denmark is such an important
theme of the play that it is in the same speech where
the new king, Claudius, speaks of grieving for his dead
brother, marrying Queen Gertrude, and thanking all
councilors and courtiers for their support and "better
wisdoms." Claudius thinks the old, bedridden, and
probably senile ruler of Norway will keep his warring
and demanding young nephew, Fortinbras, in check.
Claudius dispatches two ambassadors, Voltemand and
Cornelius, to Norway.

The king and queen move directly to another
concern; Gertrude advises Hamlet to lose his gloomy
countenance – all that lives must die, passing through
nature to eternity. (Hamlet will later extend this
observation, "To what base uses we may return,
Horatio! Why may not imagination trace the noble dust
of Alexander til 'a find it stopping a bunghole?" V.i.).
Hamlet assures his mother that his "nighted colour" is
not just an appearance. It is "that within which passeth
show" – a melancholy saturation of his person, which
may emerge in "forms, moods, and shapes of grief."
Hamlet displays a fidelity for truthfulness that is not
observed in others at court. In front of the assembled,

Claudius inappropriately lectures Hamlet that fathers die all the time, and although it is commendable to dutifully mourn his father, Hamlet's sadness has become "impious stubbornness" and "unmanly grief."

Keeping the setting in Denmark meant royal succession was based not only on birth but also on election. Hamlet later complains that Claudius had popped in between Hamlet's hopes of being King of Denmark. He was entitled to have this hope. But as Laertes later tells us, succession affects "the sanity and health of the whole state." "Madness" had been a dimension of the Hamlet character throughout much of the play's history. "That within which passeth show," threatens Hamlet's political future. Playgoers wonder if his melancholic disposition is a reason the Danish crown has passed over him. Official madness could remove him from any future election to the throne.[200] Horatio, close to Hamlet at court and at university, has seen him struggle against the disease and would doubt Hamlet's ability to win election to the throne.

Young Hamlet is more interested in returning to Wittenberg than in remaining at Elsinore. Laertes also shows good survival instincts in wanting to return to university in Paris immediately. King and queen voice their disapproval of Hamlet's intent to go back to Wittenberg, telling him they want him to remain at Elsinore in their "cheer and comfort." Gertrude prays he stay with them and not return to university. Why do Claudius and Gertrude want Hamlet to stay? Does Gertrude want him to stay because she wants to comfort him and wean him from his grief? Does Claudius fear

---

[200] On the other hand, Scot argued, "[H]e is not by conscience to be executed which hath no sound mind nor perfect judgment." Scot, *Discoverie of Witchcraft*, bk. 3, chap. 7.

Hamlet, the "most immediate to our throne," may join Fortinbras or other challenges to his throne? Does he think keeping him at court will be an easier way to keep an eye on him?

Later, when Hamlet is alone, Horatio, in the company of Marcellus and Barnardo, approaches him. While readily acknowledging the guards, whom he knows by name, Hamlet is not sure he recognizes Horatio; generously, despite some confusion, he addresses Horatio as "my good friend" and asks him, "What ... make you from Wittenberg?" Horatio answers, "A truant disposition." Hamlet does not believe this answer, so asks him in effect a third time what he's doing in Elsinore. If Horatio came for old Hamlet's funeral, it would mean he's been at court for over a month. It is odd that Horatio is still at Elsinore and odder still that a friend of Hamlet would not have already seen him at such a time.

In the same funeral/wedding exchange, a comic moment happens when Hamlet says, "My father, methinks I see my father." Horatio would be alarmed and nervously looking around to see if Osric is making an unauthorized appearance. This bit ended, Horatio gets back to the point—to get Hamlet to the guard platform to hear the ghost's request. Horatio needs to be reserved in telling Hamlet that he thinks he saw Hamlet's dead father last night; he knows Hamlet should not believe it. To season Hamlet's anticipated disbelief, he includes the witness of "these gentlemen," and some enticement: "It lifted up its head and did address [i]tself to motion like as it would speak."

Leaving aside any condolences for Hamlet's losses, what hollow Horatio does offer is that he thinks he saw Hamlet's dead father last night. This will be a tough sell. He tells Hamlet, "I knew your Father. These hands are not more like." Hamlet is troubled at Horatio's observation; one person wearing king's armor would look like another person wearing king's armor, and he asks for more details. "Armed you say?" Horatio answers again that he was armed from head to toe, "cap-a-pie." Hamlet considers this might be a bad joke but for the straight-faced mention of his dead father. Testing him further, Hamlet asks, "Then saw you not his face." Horatio eagerly assures him they saw his face because the ghost wore the helmet's beaver up. But facial details on a helmeted bearded man, even with the beaver up, could not be seen at night. The guards, Marcellus and Barnardo, stand in puzzled, awkward silence as Horatio claims to have seen what they had not seen.

Of necessity, mid-sixteenth-century Europe had moved away from full battle armor, and playgoers would have appreciated Hamlet's baffled reactions to Horatio's observations.[201] Horatio has apparently spent more time in books than in battle. The dynamic of this dialogue takes another step toward comedy when the trap-setter has a less than smooth time with the prey. Hamlet's remarks reveal a troubled curiosity about what they have seen (where was it ... did you speak to it ... 'tis very strange...), but no avowal of ghostly appearances of the departed.[202] He tests Horatio again, asking him about

---

[201] By the mid-1500s, knightly armor could be penetrated by musket fire, and soldiers needed to be quicker and more agile.

[202] And later (I.iv.), Hamlet mocks the armored impersonator of his father's ghost:
O answer me,
Let me not burst in ignorance but tell
Why thy canonized bones hearsed in death
Have burst their cerements, why the sepulcher
Wherein we saw thee quietly interred
Hath oped his ponderous and marble jaws

the ghost's expression and complexion. He puzzles that Horatio says he could see both. Here with Horatio (and later with Rosencrantz, Guildenstern, Polonius, Claudius, Ophelia and Gertrude), Hamlet knows how to draw information from people.

Hamlet agrees to watch with them, adding that maybe "it" (not "he") will walk again. Horatio guarantees him it will. The trap has been set for the ghost to reveal the murder story and ask for revenge.

As in the England of the Cecils and Walsingham, information is a valued commodity at Elsinore. Secrecy, narration, betrayal, and dishonesty are used to control others. Seeking to avoid this, Hamlet asks his informers not to tell what they've seen or what they may see that night.[203]

They leave, and Hamlet's already troubled soul is left to consider the incongruity of a ghost in full armor. Elsinore's increased concentrations on defense are common knowledge. This must leave Hamlet, a royal Dane, somewhat uneasy that guards cannot even fend off a ghost, let alone an army. He concludes all is not well and suspects foul play. Hamlet, the university student, doubts the ghost is a spiritual apparition. Still, he is not sure if the spectacle portends good or evil, if its intents be wicked or charitable. Hamlet's melancholy is not helping to clarify these uncertainties. "My father's spirit—in arms! [A]ll is not well; / I doubt [suspect] some foul play."[204]

To cast thee up again. What may this mean …

[203]   The Earl of Essex talked too much. "Essex forgot the importance of wariness in public and private utterance, unable to censor his thoughts before friends who, in a twinkling, might metamorphose into enemies." Haynes, *Invisible Power*, xiv.

[204]   "Doubt" is understood as "suspect" or "fear" in Thompson and Taylor, *Arden Shakespeare "Hamlet,"* 188, and in Jenkins, *Arden Shakespeare "Hamlet,"* 197.

In this first encounter with Hamlet, Horatio's presence at Elsinore is suspect. His honesty is questionable, as are his roles of friend and scholar. Who's there? Is Horatio there?

Act 1, scene 3

(Laertes, Ophelia, Polonius)

Act 1, scene 4

Horatio and Marcellus are joined by Hamlet on the guard platform. Unlike Horatio's earlier platform speeches (I.i.), here his utterances are reduced to strange remarks, pointing Hamlet in the direction of the trap, and interpreting the ghost's gestures for Hamlet. When Hamlet asks what time it is, he may be testing Horatio's ability to tell the truth. Horatio tells him it is not yet twelve. But the straight man, Marcellus, says it has already struck twelve. How could both Hamlet and Horatio have missed the clock striking twelve? This could be comical, with Hamlet asking this question shortly after twelve loud gongs and giving bewildered looks to Marcellus and spectators at Horatio's answer. To direct Hamlet's attention while the ghost gets into position, Horatio asks what the trumpets and noises mean. Hamlet explains to him how the king enjoys his music, dance, and drink. Even though Horatio identifies himself as "friend and liegeman to the Dane," he asks Hamlet if this noise-making is custom. These are strange questions, but ones which reveal more about Horatio's duplicity, Claudius's irresponsible kingship, and Hamlet's integrity.

Francisco has set up the mechanism or projection for the ghost to appear.[205] Horatio tells Hamlet that the ghost is appearing. In seeing the ghost, the prince responds with surprise and prayers for angels and ministers of grace to defend them. Hamlet can see that Horatio is eager for him to acknowledge the ghost and speak to it. (I remind readers that the play's List of Roles identifying the ghost as "the ghost of Hamlet's father" is a post-restoration invention. Horatio identifies the ghost as the ghost of Hamlet's father; Shakespeare does not.) Hamlet tells the ghost, since it comes in such a questionable shape, he will speak to it. Graciously, Hamlet says he will call it "Hamlet, King, father, royal Dane," but addresses the ghost with the nonparental "thou/thee" instead of "you/your."[206] He asks the ghost how the sepulcher opened its marble jaws to cast it up. He asks what it means that he, though dead, appears to them "in complete steel," forcing consideration of things "beyond the reaches of our souls."

Horatio continues to direct this play within a play; he tells Hamlet the ghost beckons him to go away with it, as if it had something to impart to Hamlet alone. The plan would be to impart the murder story to him away from anyone else's hearing. In that way, Hamlet's already weakened (rumored to be "mad") mind would bear the entire burden of the revelation with no one else to corroborate it. The mouse (Hamlet) is about to

---

[205] If the ghost is a projection, his lines could also be amplified from another area of the stage. Shakespeare may have experimented with voice-carrying techniques such as using a leaden pipe to transmit a voice across a distance. Butterworth, in *Magic on the Early English Stage*, mentions this sound technique. See 102-105. And see this book's earlier reference (chapter three) to a young William Cecil using this pipe technique as a prank to frighten a fellow student.

[206] Curiously, Hamlet switches to "your" forms to address the ghost in Act 3, scene 4.

take the bait, when straight man, Marcellus, speaks up and warns it is not a good idea to follow the ghost. But Hamlet perceives the ghost will not speak unless he goes with him, so Horatio risks a dramatic "be ruled, you shall not go" posture.

When Hamlet leaves to follow the ghost, Marcellus suggests they disobey him and follow him, but Horatio subtly dissuades him. ("Have after! To what issue will this come?") Marcellus accurately surmises that there is something rotten in the state of Denmark. Horatio responds, "Heaven will direct it." Marcellus argues that they need to follow Hamlet. A reluctant Horatio joins Marcellus.

Act 1, scene 5

The ghost moves from the initial area of the castle to the battlement parapets from which to tell Hamlet how old Hamlet was murdered.[207] (On the platform, it is a few steps for the ghost, but the outer side of the castle for Hamlet.) The battlements are high, purposely inaccessible inner castle areas with parapets and open spaces through which the ghost could appear and disappear. This could be so staged that Hamlet gives chase and finds himself just outside the castle walls, where the ghost can be seen above, through an open space in the battlements. (Later, when Horatio and Marcellus find Hamlet, they are described as "within," then they enter Hamlet's space.)

Hamlet tells the ghost to speak; Hamlet will go no further. Once alone, the ghost immediately identifies himself as his father's ghost. Why would Hamlet's

---

[207] If a reflection, projection, or mirrored image is used, this could be cast upon the initial area, then floated and cast upon or reflected from the opening in the parapet.

father's ghost have to tell Hamlet who he is? Wouldn't Hamlet have known his own father's voice?[208] Young Hamlet does not recognize the ghost as his father, and he does not act like it is his father's ghost. Although he says he will call him "father," he never does.

The ghost tells Hamlet he (the ghost) is about to burn in sulfurous tormenting flames. Hamlet responds to this overacting with "alas, poor ghost." The ghost perceives Hamlet's doubt, so tells Hamlet to listen seriously to what he has to tell him. Hamlet tells him to speak—that's why Hamlet is there. The ghost bewails his tragic state, then tries, "if thou didst ever thy dear father love." To this, Hamlet gives the frustrated, eye-rolling reply, "Oh God!" Finally, the ghost gets to the point: he wants the prince to revenge "his foul and most unnatural murder." Incongruous though his form may be, he now has Hamlet's full attention. Hamlet had already suspected that his father's death was not an accident. "Murder!" repeats Hamlet. Hamlet himself could have spoken the ghost's long and hateful rant regarding the usurping, incestuous, adulterate beast, Claudius. The ghost asks Hamlet to revenge Claudius's awful deeds without tainting his own mind. The ghost's curious urging not to harm or contrive against Gertrude, but to leave her to heaven, echoes the advice Horatio has just given Marcellus, "heaven will direct it." This time, Hamlet's exclamation, "O all you host of heaven," after the ghost's "adieu, remember me," is voiced in anguish.

The ghost feels compelled to leave at once. As he is lowered into the cellarage (or as his reflection vanishes, while his voice in the cellarage remains), he

---

[208]   Martin Scofield asks this question, too, in *The Ghosts of Hamlet*, 33.

repeatedly warns our melancholic, distracted Hamlet to remember him.

Horatio and Marcellus enter Hamlet's space. Their conversations become strange again. Hamlet does not know if he can trust anyone. He is beginning to recognize the murder story as a story that he and Horatio already know from the theater. He needs time to contemplate the message and the messenger. The official story given out was that old Hamlet had died of a serpent sting—"So the whole ear of Denmark / Is by a forged process of my death / Rankly abused." That his father's death was a murder, not an accident, sinks daggers into every fiber of his already weakened self. It will be enough to discover the truth of the message, let alone identify the means of revelation. Hamlet does not know what is behind the strange messenger and ponders the authenticity of a father who would come back from the dead to ask his son to murder. Unlike Horatio, Hamlet is not ready to discard Protestant teachings that ghosts are diabolical deceptions and that the dead do not come back from the grave. But he'll suspend disbelief. He'll wipe away all learned and educated hindrances to understanding and remembering what the ghost has told him. Avenging his father's murder will have to be the "volume of his brain." Hamlet's aim shifts from curiosity about someone in armor posing as his father, to confirming that Claudius murdered his father.

Hamlet's first inclination is that the ghost could be a devilish means to get him to "couple hell," and he answers Horatio and Marcellus's curiosity about what happened with a curiosity. He says his news is "wonderful," and teases them with a secret probably well-known in Elsinore: "There never was a villain dwelling in all Denmark, but he's an arrant knave." Horatio has gone to a lot of trouble to get this obtuse, probably insulting reply. Disappointed, Horatio says, "There needs no ghost, my lord, come from the grave to tell us this." Hamlet replies Horatio is right about that. This exchange is in all three texts.

As courteously as possible, Hamlet tells them, in effect, to get about their own business while he, for his part, goes to pray.[209] Horatio, obviously annoyed, tells him these are "wild and whirling words." Hamlet says he's sorry his words offend him. Horatio quickly denies the offense, but Hamlet assures him there is offense in what he has said. He tells them it has been an honest ghost, and the meaning Hamlet holds to himself is that the ghost has *spoken* honestly about Claudius. Hamlet's response to the "old mole" in the cellarage confirms that he knows the ghost has been a show of conjuring. He plays along. "Hic et ubique" are jugglers' (magicians') terms to grace and adorn actions, the more to astonish onlookers.[210]

At this point in the *Hamlet*-esque *Bestrafte Brudermord*, Hamlet tells Horatio of his father's death, and Horatio in turn assures Hamlet of his loyalty.[211] But Shakespeare's *Hamlet* has no such exchange. (At

---

[209] "[Hamlet] leaves his companions of the night-watch to go and pray, prayer accompanied with fasting, according to the recognised precepts of Protestant pastors, since as [Ludwig] Lavater writes: 'It behoueth them which are vexed with spirits, to pray especially, and to [give] themselves to fasting, sobrietie, watching and [upright] and godly [living].'" Wilson, *What Happens in "Hamlet,"* 73.

[210] Butterworth, *Magic on the Early English Stage*, 85. Butterworth references Reginald Scot here.

[211] Greg informs us the *Bestrafte Brudermord* is the early German play, based on some version acted by the English companies touring in Germany. Greg, "Hamlet's Hallucination," 398.

some point, possibly in a scene lost to surviving texts, Hamlet tells Horatio something of the king's death, because in Act 3, scene 2, he tells Horatio: "One scene comes near the circumstance which I have told thee, of my father's death.") Again, he asks Marcellus and Horatio never to make known what they have seen tonight. He is not sure what might be reported back to the king and queen. When they say they will not make known what they have seen, he asks them to swear it. Then, from below the stage as written in all three texts, the theatrical ghost's voice joins in on the request to swear secrecy. The ghost itself could be visible to some spectators if the curtains are open in the below-stage area.[212] Hamlet mocks the pretender, unavoidably letting the audience know that he regards the ghost as knavery and not as his father's body cast up from the sepulcher's marbled jaws.[213] Horatio comments how "wondrous strange" this is. Hamlet strikes back at the value of Horatio's scholarship and adds that since Horatio is a stranger (foreigner) himself, he should welcome strange.

As a cover for uncertainties and melancholy, Hamlet tells them that if he should behave oddly or strangely, he's just putting on an antic disposition, and they are not to let on to anyone that they think he is crazy. Bradley argues, "That Hamlet was not far from insanity is very probable. His adoption of the pretence of madness may well have been due in part to fear of the reality;

---

[212]   In a 1606 essay Thomas Dekker writes, "Hell being vnder euerie one of their Stages, the Players ... might with a false Trappe doore haue flipt him downe, and there kept him, as a laughing stocke to al their yawning Spectators." *The Non-Dramatic Works of Thomas Dekker*, 5 vols., Alexander Grosart, ed. (London: Huth, 1885), vol. 2, 92.

[213]   See pages 90-91 in Janette Dillon's *Cambridge Introduction to Early English Theatre*.

to an instinct of self-preservation, a fore-feeling that
the pretence would enable him to give some utterance
to the load that pressed on his heart and brain, and
a fear that he would be unable altogether to repress
such utterance. ... [T]o use the word 'disease' loosely,
Hamlet's condition may truly be called diseased. No
exertion of will could have dispelled it."[214] Wilson also
writes that Shakespeare "wishes us to feel that Hamlet
assumes madness because he cannot help it."[215] What
better cover for madness than telling them that when
he appears mad, he is just pretending? Even someone
who is mad can put on an antic disposition, maybe
especially one who is mad. Hamlet needed to disguise
his melancholy while struggling with other weighty
burdens.

Too many revelations come to Hamlet at once.
Someone is trying to trick this university student and
grieving son with a medieval (smoke and mirrors?)
ghost, but the story about how his father was murdered
by Claudius, despite its source, is a believable call to
action. Hamlet's tasks are many. How does he test the
murder story told to him alone from a source that can
neither be summoned nor corroborated? How does he,
a person of conscience, resolve to murder someone —
especially as this could send Hamlet to prison, the
block, hell, or all three? How does he, a royal public
figure and most immediate to the throne, nobly deal
with these challenges while burdened with melancholy,
emotional instability, and a lack of people he can trust?

---

[214] A. C. Bradley, *Shakespearean Tragedy: Lectures on Hamlet, Othello,
King Lear, Macbeth*, 2nd ed. (London: Macmillan, 1905), 120-121. Also
see Greg's footnote, page 417, in "Hamlet's Hallucination."

[215] Wilson, *What Happens in "Hamlet,"* 92.

Taillepied's words predict Hamlet's struggle: "The evil Spirit goes about seeking whom he may devour, and should he chance to find a man already of melancholic … humor, who on account of some great loss, or haply because he deems his honor tarnished, the demon here has a fine field to his hand, and he will tempt the poor wretch to depths of misery and depression."[216] Horatio anticipates that Hamlet's melancholy will make him an easier target. But Horatio and Hamlet (and scholarly playgoers) have read that if a ghost appears to a melancholic, the ghost is demonic.[217] Using reverse logic, if Hamlet wants to assert that the ghost is not demonic, he would also need to assert that he is not mad, just pretending to be. ("Manie thorough melancholie doo imagine, that they see or heare visions, spirits, ghosts, strange noises …"[218])

The information the ghost provides Hamlet is clear. But why would this troubling information need to come from the mouth of an informer disguised as the ghost of his dead father, who, Hamlet knows, rests in that "undiscovered country from whose bourn, no traveller returns" (III.i.)? Hamlet understands the revelation of murder, but he is not sure who hides behind the revelation. Nor does he know if the informer means well or ill. Someone is pretending to be his father's ghost while the professed "poor servant ever," Horatio, is going along with it. Hamlet alternates between paralyzed shock and confused outrage.

---

[216] Arthur F. Kinney, ed., "Hamlet": New Critical Essays, page 16, from Noel Taillepied's Treatise of Ghosts (1588).

[217] Wilson, What Happens in "Hamlet," Appendix E, 309-320, regarding Timothy Bright's A Treatise on Melancholy, (1586).

[218] Scot, Discoverie of Witchcraft, bk. 15, chap. 39.

Fear, distrust, and betrayal — defining patterns in Tudor England — also motivate actions at Elsinore. Johnston's words aptly set the mood.

> [E]lsinore is a deceptive world. One can never be sure whether someone is spying or eavesdropping. Elsinore is full of nooks, arrases, upper galleries where someone may be lurking in secret. It's a place where you have to keep your wits about you if you want to survive. When someone approaches you with a smile on his face, you can never be sure whether he is a friend or a foe, whether what he is saying to you is what he really means or whether it is all just a temporary role he is playing in this dangerous and duplicitous game.[219]

Act 2, scene 1

Through the sly abuse of information, Polonius relates to Shakespeare's contemporaries in the Elizabethan spy service. (See Chapter 2, "The Cecils.") He instructs a court spy, Reynaldo, how to gather information on Polonius's son, Laertes, while Laertes is away in Paris. This lengthy scene emphasizes that deception and stealth are status quo for gathering and disseminating information at Elsinore. This scene also puts Reynaldo in the powerful position of knowing some ins and outs of court intrigue, making his a key stage presence for the director and giving spectators reason to watch what Reynaldo does and whose company he keeps.

After Reynaldo leaves, a frightened Ophelia enters the room. Following her father Polonius's command, Ophelia has not accepted Hamlet's letters or company. She tells her father of an unusual and poignant encounter with Hamlet, who entered her room while she was sewing.

---

[219] Johnston, "Introductory Lecture on Shakespeare's *Hamlet*," pt. D., "Appearance and Reality."

Act 2, scene 2

This, the longest scene in *Hamlet,* focuses on discovering various characters' dispositions. Claudius and Gertrude send Rosencrantz and Guildenstern to find out what is going on with Hamlet, and Hamlet, in turn, finds out why Rosencrantz and Guildenstern are there. Voltemand delivers a (false) report from Norway about what Fortinbras intends. Horatio is identified to spectators as Osric's helper from Act 1, scene 1. Polonius proposes an explanation for Hamlet's madness by showing the king and queen Hamlet's love letters obtained ("through her duty and obedience") from Ophelia. To test the ghost's message, Hamlet coaches the players to perform a play that he hopes will cause Claudius to confess to murder.

About two months have passed since Act 1. This scene opens with a "flourish" (the second of the play's three flourishes), as the king and queen enter accompanied by Rosencrantz, Guildenstern, "and other Courtiers."[220] Horatio and Osric are among these courtiers, and they stand together. Horatio wears an item of clothing, or displays an action or item, to identify him as Osric's helper from the play's opening scene (I.i.). Horatio exits with Voltemand just before Polonius's "This business is well ended" at line 85.

King and queen have sent for Hamlet's childhood friends, Rosencrantz and Guildenstern, to discuss the "transformation" in Gertrude's "too much changed son." This scene echoes the beginning of the preceding scene, where Claudius asks the friends, in attendance

---

[220]   Later, in line 36, the queen will address "some of you," to imply a group. And after the king's "Most welcome home," line 85, Voltemand and Cornelius exit with other courtiers.

of "others," to draw Hamlet on to pleasures and to gather as much information from him as they can.

Polonius enters with news that the ambassadors to Norway have returned and that he already knows the cause of "Hamlet's lunacy." Voltemand gives his report from Norway. He reports that Norway stopped his nephew, Fortinbras, from issuing levies to pay for what Norway thought was war against the Polack but were actually to pay for war against King Claudius. He reports that Norway, in sickness and old age, was so grieved at his nephew's action that he sent out an arrest on young Fortinbras. Voltemand continues that Fortinbras received rebuke from Norway and gave Norway his vow that he would never more try to raise war funds against Claudius. Voltemand reports Norway was so overjoyed at Fortinbras's transformation that he gave Fortinbras money, retention of the soldiers he had raised, and with Claudius's permission, a campaign through Denmark to battle the Polack.

Having seen how matters of intelligence are handled, even against one's own family, why would anyone trust the information delivered by Voltemand?[221] His report would likely contain deception from others and/or from himself. The deception we witness at Elsinore would not be limited to Elsinore. Old Norway could have deceived, or the bedridden old man may have (yet again) been deceived by young Fortinbras. The campaign through Denmark is a ruse to allow Fortinbras an armed presence in Denmark. In Q1's final scene, Voltemar (Voltemand) enters at the same time

---

[221] "Robert Beale, an official of government close to Walsingham wrote: 'Be not too credulous lest you be deceived; hear all reports but trust not all; weigh them with time and deliberation and be not too liberal with trifles; observe them that deal on both hands lest you be deceived.'" Alford, *The Watchers*, 313.

as Fortinbras. I would cast Voltemand (one who turns) as a double agent working with Fortinbras against Claudius. (See this book's section, "Inventors' Heads.")

It suits Claudius's nature to accept the report instead of questioning it. In all three texts, he responds to this effect: "It likes us well, and at fit time and leasure weele reade and answere these his Articles." King for only months, he takes the report handed him by Voltemand, sets it aside, and reaches instead for his wine goblet. (Claudius prefers to "take his rouse," drink, and be with the woman who is conjunctive to his life and soul.) Polonius butters this response by proclaiming the "business is well ended." We never see Claudius respond to the articles. He puts off this Fortinbras business, and before the ambassadors leave, he invites all to a feast that night. According to Hamlet, revelry, "more honored in the breach than the observance," is the custom and has reduced Denmark's standing among other nations (I.iv.). Voltemand exits with Horatio, Osric, Cornelius, and other courtiers.

Claudius is also distracted by his need to control his angry, popular, and unpredictable nephew, who he has (probably to his regret) publicly stated is the most immediate to the throne. Managing that concern, as Polonius misstates it, is like the great feast to which the news from Norway is but a sweet portion.

Polonius tells Claudius and Gertrude their noble son is mad and shows them love letters Hamlet has written to Ophelia. Hamlet reveals in a letter the one thing he knows for sure at Elsinore: his love for Ophelia. Polonius claims the cause of Hamlet's madness is his lack of access to Ophelia. If this is not the cause, Polonius offers his head. But lines later, more cautiously, he offers to resign his position. In another act of deception, Polonius proposes that he and Claudius set up a meeting between the two lovers and then hide to eavesdrop. Hamlet himself is within earshot of this part of the conversation: he comes upon them while they are bent over his letters but backs out of sight when he hears what they are discussing.

Later in the scene, when Rosencrantz and Guildenstern meet Hamlet, he informs them Denmark is a prison. Echoing his opening question to Horatio, he asks Rosencrantz and Guildenstern, "What make you at Elsinore?" Echoing Horatio, they hedge about why they are there. Hamlet reminds them of the obligation of "their ever-preserved love," and after some hesitation they agree to tell him they had been sent for.[222] Hamlet tells them he anticipates the reason they were sent for, and tells them outright what afflicts him. His description (lines 261-276) sounds like a list of symptoms from *A Treatise on Melancholy* by Timothy Bright, printed in 1586.[223]

The play fleshes out a victim of melancholy/madness in the character of Hamlet. Shakespeare had probably known the effects of melancholy.[224] People in the late sixteenth into the seventeenth century gave much thought to this malady; the age was beginning to view melancholy less as demonic possession and more as a

---

[222]   Gertrude praises Rosencrantz and Guildenstern (II.i. 20-21). She is sure that "two men there is not living to whom [Hamlet] more adheres."

[223]   *A Treatise on Melancholy* (1586) by Timothy Bright, a protégé of Walsingham. Shakespeare was apparently familiar with this work, which was well known at the time Shakespeare was writing *Hamlet*. See also *What Happens in "Hamlet"* for Wilson's Appendix E: "Shakespeare's Knowledge of *A Treatise on Melancholy* by Timothy Bright," 309-320.

[224]   John J. Ross, "Shakespeare's Chancre: Did the Bard have Syphilis?" *Clinical Infectious Diseases* 40, no. 3 (1 Feb 2005): 399-404.

recognizable disease process with a list of symptoms.[225] The playwright would have been familiar with the growing interest and publications on melancholy and would have seen how those who suffered it were misunderstood and abused. Wilson believed that Shakespeare himself was subject to a mood of gloom and dejection that brought him near madness.[226]

This disease frustrates Hamlet's ability to respond to multiple challenges received in too rapid succession:

his illness

his father's death

being passed over for the throne of Denmark, in favor of his uncle, Claudius

his mother's immediate remarriage to Claudius

not returning to Wittenberg as wished

the ghostly revelation that his father was murdered by his mother's new husband, King Claudius

the ghost's charge to murder Claudius

the inaccessible means through which the murder story is communicated, precluding summoning or cross-examination of the "witness"

the necessity of rejecting his lover, Ophelia

feeling that he is a prisoner in his own home

being spied upon by friends

the inability to know who can be trusted and a growing awareness that no one at Elsinore can be trusted

---

[225] Caroline Spurgeon writes that disease and corruption—a "hidden corruption infecting and destroying a wholesome body"—dominate the play and that Hamlet's condition, for which he is not to blame, is the tragedy of *Hamlet*. This condition "in its course and development, impartially and relentlessly, annihilates him and others, innocent and guilty alike." Spurgeon, *Shakespeare's Imagery and What It Tells Us* (Cambridge: Cambridge University Press, 1935), 213, 318-319.

[226] Wilson, *The Essential Shakespeare*, 115.

Johann Wolfgang von Goethe, in *Wilhelm Meister's Apprenticeship*, describes Hamlet's plight as an oak tree planted in a costly/precious flower pot. The roots expand and the pot shatters.[227]

In the two months between seeing the ghost and speaking his "to be or not to be" soliloquy, Hamlet has prayed, fasted, and written love letters, but he has not killed Claudius. This has been enough time for a troupe of actors to travel to Elsinore. Rosencrantz and Guildenstern correctly anticipate that Hamlet will brighten at this news. The players arrive and Polonius enters, too. Hamlet tells the players he chiefly loved a speech in one of their plays that speaks of Priam's slaughter. The story is from Virgil's *Aeneid*. (See Robert Fagles' 2006 translation, pages 74-84.) Pyrrhus wants to avenge his father's death and hides inside the Trojan gift horse to surreptitiously enter Troy and brutally slay King Priam. The Trojan horse is the trick to smuggle Greek soldiers into Troy's fortress where they kill the guards and open the gates to the waiting Greek army. The tale points to Elsinore: the ghost trick, Fortinbras's army, and the ensuing destruction of Denmark's kingdom from within.

To test the ghost's story, Hamlet asks the players to perform *The Murder of Gonzago*. The dumb show will play out the murder of old Hamlet as narrated by the ghost. As Wilson writes, "The ghost's story and the Gonzago story are one, except in ... trivial particulars ... [and] this coincidence is deliberate."[228] How does

---

[227] "Hier wird ein Eichbaum in ein koestliches Gefaess gepflanzt, das nur liebliche Blumen in seinen Schoss haette aufnehmen sollen; die Wurzeln dehnen sich aus, das Gefaess wird zernichtet." (J. W. von Goethe, *Wilhelm Meisters Lehrjahre*, 1795-96, bk. 4, chap. 13.)

[228] But Wilson writes that we are not supposed to dwell on this. If we do, "we are faced with the fact that the players arrive at Elsinore with an item in their repertory which embodies a detailed account of

it happen that the method of murder in the Gonzago play is the same as the method of murder narrated by the ghost?[229] Hamlet, having knowledge of the theater, is familiar with the Gonzago play, and it must seem strange to him that the play tells the ghost's story, except that in *Gonzago*, it is the nephew who kills the king.

Hamlet concludes that the spirit he has seen may be a devil. His remaining energies and wits now focus on verifying the story of the murder of his father. It suits Hamlet's nature to question the reliability of testimony from a ghost who, by the way, has not bothered to put in another appearance in the despairing months Hamlet has had to consider its plea for revenge. He cannot simply follow the ghost's bidding. The philosopher G. W. F. Hegel sees Hamlet's questioning disbelief in the ghost as a profound character trait, which "lets his revenge tarry for the revelation which the spirit of his father makes regarding the crime that did him to death ... for reason that the spirit giving the revelation might possibly be the devil."[230]

---

the assassination of King Hamlet, an account which must have been written before the crime actually took place. And yet three centuries of spectators and readers have found no difficulty in swallowing the coincidence; they have been conscious of it, otherwise the play scene would have lost ... its meaning, but they have seen nothing strange or incredible in it." Wilson, *What Happens in "Hamlet,"* 141.

[229] In a footnote, Greg also points out that the story may have had some underpinnings in historical fact. He quotes Dowden's *Hamlet* (1899), "In 1538 the Duke of Urbino, married to a Gonzaga, was murdered by a Luigi Gonzaga, who dropped poison into his ear." Greg, "Hamlet's Hallucination," 397.

[230] Georg Friedrich Wilhelm Hegel, *On Tragedy*, eds. Anne Paolucci and Henry Paolucci (Westport, CT: Greenwood Publishing, 1978) 294-5.

Act 3, scene 1

We see more lessons in deception from Polonius and Claudius: they put Ophelia in Hamlet's path, instructing her to read a book. "With devotion's visage and pious action we do sugar o'er the devil himself." They hide to eavesdrop and to be "seeing unseen." Hamlet loves Ophelia, but Gertrude's son is ill, "rank and gross in nature." He leaves Ophelia no doubt that he cannot marry her. He tells her that if she does marry, she'll bring this burden with her as her dowry.[231] What children could they hope for save a brood of sinners? He clearly communicates to Ophelia that she needs to be celibate, and her best recourse is to enter a nunnery. *Hamlet* is not a case study in nerve disease, but by staging a walking case of melancholy in the struggling yet relatively likeable character of one burdened by

---

[231] Hamlet's descriptions of his melancholy resemble some signs and symptoms of syphilis. Syphilis, known then by other names such as "the pox" or "the infinite malady," was widespread in Shakespeare's England. In 1579, a physician at St. Bartholomew's Hospital in London claimed that 75 percent of the patients had the "French Pox" (J. Fabricius, *Syphilis in Shakespeare's England*, London: Jessica Kingsley, 1994).

By the late sixteenth century, symptoms of syphilis and melancholy were linked. Descriptions of the stages of the pox (syphilis) were clear by Shakespeare's time: contagion, skin manifestations, body ulcerations, and intense head and bone pain (Claude Quetel, *History of Syphilis*, trans. J. Braddock and B. Pike, Baltimore: Johns Hopkins University Press, 1992).

Melancholy was thought to cause syphilis and syphilis was thought to cause melancholy. Melancholy, syphilis, and madness were major and interchangeable manifestations (Greg Bentley, "Melancholy, Madness, and Syphilis" in *Hamlet, Hamlet Studies*, 6.1-2 (1984): 75-80).

Quoting several medical studies, Ross writes that "[u]p to 85% of patients with venereal disease have psychological symptoms including anger, anxiety, depression, sexual dysfunction, and misogyny." Shakespeare's writings are more preoccupied with venereal disease than the writings of his contemporaries, and some have suggested Shakespeare himself had syphilis. (John J. Ross, "Shakespeare's Chancre: Did the Bard Have Syphilis?" 399-404.)

nerve disease, the playwright deepens spectators' understanding of mental illness (versus witchcraft) and increases empathy for Hamlet.

After Hamlet tells Ophelia there will be "no moe marriage," the (printer's?) stage direction (in F1 and Q2) reads "Exit," but Hamlet only pretends to leave. He lingers to the side of the stage, possibly hiding behind a statue of a cherub, and watches to see that Ophelia is all right. Polonius and Claudius are facing away from him. He hears the king's plan that Hamlet "shall with speed to England." At Polonius's "How now, Ophelia," she turns toward the king and her father, and Hamlet completes his exit before they see him.

Act 3, scene 2

For the second time in the play, Hamlet seems surprised to see Horatio, with his "What ho, Horatio!" at line 49. Has Horatio been there throughout the scene but partially hidden? Has he just appeared out of nowhere?

Hamlet describes Horatio (lines 50-70), as one who takes Fortune's buffets and rewards with equal thanks; he is not passion's slave. Hamlet tells him that nothing seems to bother him. Horatio is dispassionate, suffers nothing, accepts bad and good with indifference (equal thanks), and will not be played upon. These lines are generally heard as compliments, but these could also be a list of developmental weaknesses in one with limited compassion. Hamlet anticipates Horatio will hear these words neither as praise nor as weaknesses. He pauses after "Dost thou hear?" — Horatio has no response. He pauses again after "I will wear him in my heart's core" — Horatio makes no response. He rephrases, "ay, in my heart of heart" — and waits, but still no response.

Finally, speaking clearly, as to a foreign speaker, he emphasizes, "As I do thee." Horatio, as if deaf, can offer no reply in kind. Said virtues are like notes beyond Horatio's hearing range. In Shakespeare's *Henry V*, written in the same time period, a conspirator's virtues are listed in a similar manner at the same time the former friend's treachery is revealed.[232] Hamlet could no more be the dispassionate, calculating, all-information-no-emotion Horatio than Horatio could be the sensitive, truth-seeking, emotionally complicated Hamlet.

Hamlet tells him that the king will see a play tonight that comes near the circumstance of Hamlet's father's death.[233] Hamlet has heard that guilty people have been

---

[232]   Thompson and Taylor, *Arden Shakespeare "Hamlet,"* 300.
    And see *Henry V*, Act 2, scene 2. This is an abbreviated excerpt: "What shall I say to thee ... thou that didst bear the key of all my counsels, that knew'st the very bottom of my soul, That (almost) mightst have coined me into gold, Wouldst thou have practiced on me, for thy use? ... [O]r are [men] spare in diet, free from gross passion or of mirth, or anger, constant in spirit, not swerving with the blood, garnished and decked in modest complement, not working with the eye without the ear, and but in purged judgment trusting neither? Such and so finely bolted didst thou seem: and thus thy fall hath left a kind of blot to mark the full-fraught man and best indued with some suspicion. I will weep for thee. For this revolt of thine, methinks, is like another fall of man. ... Their faults are open, arrest them." (*The Complete Works of William Shakespeare*, Masters Library ser., London: Octopus Books; Minneapolis: Amaranth, 1985, 465.)

[233]   Greg suggests the story the ghost tells Hamlet about the murder is untrue. Greg allows that Claudius killed old Hamlet, as Claudius admits to this, but he says the poison in the ear story is a lie, a duplication of a plot in a play already known to Hamlet. [If Hamlet knows this Italian play from Wittenberg, I assert Horatio knows it as well.] Greg argues, "It must strike the reader that, if Claudius really poisoned his brother in the manner described by the Ghost, it is unbelievable that the players should chance to have in stock a play, which not only reproduced so closely the general situation, but in which the murderer adopted just this exceptional method by which to dispatch his victim." He goes on to say that the reason Claudius puts an abrupt end to the play is because he is now convinced that Hamlet

so struck to the soul by a cunning theater scene that they proclaim their misdeeds (II.ii. 523-527).[234] He asks Horatio to join him in watching Claudius for signs of guilt. Hamlet concludes that if the king's guilt does not "itself unkennel in one speech, it is a damned ghost" that they have seen and his "imaginations are as foul."

Earlier (in all three texts), Hamlet has asked the players to insert 12-16 lines into the play. We must guess which lines Hamlet inserted into the play. The following lines, followed by "But orderly to end where I begun," could have been directed at Horatio:

[E]ven our loves should with our fortunes change,
For 'tis a question left us yet to prove,
Whether love lead fortune or else fortune love.
The great man down, you mark his favourite flies;
The poor advanced makes friends of enemies;
And hitherto doth love on fortune tend,
For who not needs shall never lack a friend;
And who in want a hollow friend doth try,
Directly seasons him his enemy.
But orderly to where I begun, ...

When the crown passes over Hamlet, it weakens Horatio's standing at court. "Our loves should with our fortunes [no crown] change." And we recall Francis Bacon, a favorite of Essex, when we hear, "the great man down [Hamlet or Essex], you mark his favourite [Horatio or Bacon] flies." Earlier, when Hamlet asks Horatio, "Nay, do not think I flatter, [f]or

is not only mad but dangerous and must quickly be sent away. See Greg's "Hamlet's Hallucination," 403.

[234] "A widow confesses in this way to having murdered her husband in the anonymous play, *A Warning for Fair Women*, which was acted by Shakespeare's company in 1599." Thompson and Taylor, *Arden Shakespeare "Hamlet*," 278.

what advancement may I hope from thee [t]hat no revenue hast but thy good spirits," he foretells "the poor [Horatio] advanced makes friends of enemies [Fortinbras]." And "who in want [Hamlet] a hollow friend [Horatio] doth try, directly seasons him his enemy."

King Claudius abruptly stops the Gonzago play after the nephew pours poison into the player king's ears. Hamlet tells Horatio that he will take the ghost's word for a thousand pound.[235] He asks Horatio if he perceived. Horatio gives less than resounding affirmations with, "Very well, my lord," and "I did very well note him." Their discussion is interrupted by Rosencrantz and Guildenstern, who have come to let Hamlet know his uncle is angry, and the queen wants to see Hamlet in her room.[236] Horatio is present for these discussions with Rosencrantz, Guildenstern, and the players. He's there when Polonius repeats Gertrude's request to speak with Hamlet in her room. Hearing all of this, Horatio would not have just gone to bed. Rosencrantz and Guildenstern dutifully exit at Hamlet's "Leave me, friends," but not Horatio. He lingers to the side and is pleased to hear Hamlet say, "Now could I drink hot blood / And do such bitter business as the day / Would quake to look on."

Meanwhile, on a side stage, spectators see Osric very annoyed that the night's entertainment has been cut short. To punctuate Hamlet's "For some must watch while some must sleep" (line 265), Osric puts

---

[235] When the king cuts short *The Murder of Gonzago*, Claudius's agitation in shutting down the play could have been because Hamlet was out of control, or because he feared the audience would suspect him, or because he didn't like the threatening nature of the play, especially given Hamlet is his nephew. See Scofield, *The Ghosts of Hamlet*, 60.

[236] The text refers to the queen's room as the queen's closet.

on his nightshirt and cap, blows out the candle, and gets into bed.

Rosencrantz and Guildenstern go to the king, where Polonius will join them. When all except Hamlet exit, Horatio secretly waits to follow him.

Act 3, scene 3

Optimistic that Hamlet is finally fired up enough to kill Claudius, Horatio follows him. Hamlet fails to be predictable and walks past the opportunity to kill Claudius. When Horatio sees that Hamlet does not kill the king, it is time to call in the ghost to remind Hamlet he is supposed to kill Claudius. After all, the intended but reluctant assassin, Prince Hamlet, will soon be shipped off to England. Exasperated, Horatio rushes to find Osric who, on a side stage, in view of spectators, has gone to bed in a huff. Critics have puzzled over the stage direction, "in his nightgown," for Osric's appearance in the following scene. This could be comical—Osric does not have time to put on heavy armor and sprint off to the landing outside the queen's portal. He must appear in his nightgown. He attaches and fluffs the sable-silvered beard, pulls the nightcap over as much of his face as possible, dusts himself with ashes, and hastens with Horatio to the portal outside the queen's room.

Act 3, scene 4

The setting is the queen's room, probably an upper room in the castle. There needs to be an opening, recessed deeply into the castle wall, through which the ghost (the actual actor or the reflected image) would be seen. At the ghost's appearance, Hamlet asks protection from heavenly guards.

As explained earlier, Hamlet sees and hears the ghost, but his mother says she does not. After Hamlet kills Polonious, the queen naturally becomes more alarmed and defensive. Four times she begs him to speak no more. Then, fearing for her life and tormented by Hamlet's accusations, she sobs, "No more," cowers, and covers her head and ears, probably grabbing pillows to do so. When the ghost speaks from the portal, she does not hear it, because she has covered her ears.[237] Dialogue constitutes the evidence: she has begged at least four times for Hamlet to stop berating her; she has pillows at arm's length and finally covers her ears. She tries to uncover her ears once, but Hamlet appears to be in frightened conversation with, from her perspective, the air. She says, "alas he's mad," cowers, and covers her head and ears again. If Gertrude saw or heard the ghost, she could affirm that the appearance is not her dead husband. While Gertrude cowers, Horatio coaches the ghost to hiss out admonishments to Hamlet. The ghost's last words are "speak to her," and Hamlet gently pulls Gertrude's hands and arms away from her ears. Before Gertrude can get in position to see the ghost, it "steals away."

The emotionally charged closet scene could also add some levity and create solid, consequential actions to underscore characters' lines. It could create layered stories for spectators, leaving mixed understandings of the scene.

---

[237]   Regarding portal (doorway), Thompson and Taylor write, "[T]his explicit reference, found in all three texts, makes it clear that in the original staging, the Ghost did not use a trapdoor at this point but left by one of the usual stage doors ..." *Arden Shakespeare "Hamlet,"* 347.

Hamlet reveals to his mother that he knows he's supposed to be sent to England. He knows this from listening to Claudius and Polonius at the end of Act 3, scene 1. But his rattled mother isn't sure how he knows this and answers with an evasive, "Alack, I had forgot ..." Hamlet has murdered Polonius and this puts Hamlet on the fast track to England. The ghost is never mentioned again.

Q1 Act 3, scene 4

In the Q1 text, Hamlet tells his mother that his father was murdered, and she says she knew nothing of it. She vows by the majesty that knows our thoughts and looks into our hearts that she will conceal, consent, and do her best to go along with whatever strategy Hamlet devises.

Act 4, scene 1

(King and Queen, Rosencrantz and Guildenstern)

Act 4, scene 2

(Hamlet, Rosencrantz and Guildenstern; Francisco is included among "others")

Act 4, scene 3

(King, Rosencrantz, Guildenstern, Hamlet, Attendants, "all the rest" — Horatio, Marcellus, Francisco, Osric, and others)

Act 4, scene 4

(Fortinbras, Hamlet, Captain, Rosencrantz, Guildenstern, others)

Hamlet is accompanied by Rosencrantz and Guildenstern on his way to voyage to England. Fortinbras takes stage with his army and a captain. Only a couple of days after Voltemand's report to Claudius, Fortinbras is already in Denmark, and Hamlet is surprised to see foreign troops in Denmark without Danish accompaniment.[238] Fortinbras seems to have set out before hearing Claudius's agreement and in using the royal pronoun to refer to himself, "seems to consider himself a conquering king."[239]

Fortinbras has lines in only two scenes — this scene and the last (V.ii.). He instructs his captain to go and tell the Danish king that Fortinbras and his army are following through on the "promised march over his kingdom." Invading Poland is the ruse to get Fortinbras and his army in position to storm and occupy Elsinore. Fortinbras reminds the captain of the rendezvous, a point to gather outside Elsinore. The captain meets the passed over Danish king, Hamlet. Showing good king sense, Hamlet strategically asks the captain whose troops (powers) these are, what their purpose is, who commands them, and what they hope to achieve. The captain is evasive, claiming they are only after a small patch of ground that has no profit in it but its name. Hamlet questions why so many troops are needed, believing no one would defend the loss of men ("fight for a plot whereon the numbers cannot try the cause"). The captain assures him the other side has already

---

[238]   Blits, *Deadly Thought*, 271.

[239]   Blits, *Deadly Thought*, 271.

garrisoned thousands of men to defend it. The inquiry is cut short. Since Rosencrantz and Guildenstern were ordered to "tempt [Hamlet] with speed abroad, delay it not," they are annoyed that Hamlet has taken time to converse with the captain, and urge, "Will it please you go, my lord?"

Act 4, scene 5

With Horatio present, the gentleman describes Ophelia's apparent mental decline to the queen; he says Ophelia's words "carry but half sense" and urges Gertrude to speak to her. Consistently taking an intelligence position, Horatio advises that it would be "good she were spoken with," not because she is unwell, but because she may have information ("dangerous conjectures"), which Horatio does not want public ("in ill-breeding minds"). The queen and king see Ophelia "[d]ivided from herself and her fair judgement." When Ophelia leaves, the king asks Horatio to "[f]ollow her close; give her good watch, I pray you."

This scene directly contrasts Ophelia's madness with Hamlet's ability to reason, as witnessed in the previous scene. And though Hamlet remains lucid enough to recognize and describe his madness, Ophelia's madness becomes so extreme that her words do not recognize or describe it. Hamlet's melancholy is more a burdensome distraction in contrast to Ophelia's sudden, unapproachable, and inconsolable insanity. Her last "sane" words are "The King rises." These are spoken during the Gonzago play in remark to Claudius's action after the nephew pours poison into the ear of the player king (III.ii.). Her madness has progressed so quickly, that one has to wonder if she has consumed something (self-administered or other-administered) to speed her release from Elsinore. Elsinore's court is well acquainted with poisons, and perhaps this is an understood action in the play. In the last scene of Act I, the ghost tells Hamlet a lethal dose of the "juice of cursed hebona" was poured into the old king's ears. Pliny speaks of pouring oil of henbane into the ears to produce mental derangement.[240]

Laertes comes to the king and queen, angry about his father's murder. Ophelia reenters while he is there. Where is Horatio, who is supposed to be giving her good watch? Does he accompany her? Laertes witnesses her madness and says, "O rose of May, / Dear maid, kind sister, sweet Ophelia, / O heavens, is't possible a young maid's wits / Should be as mortal as a poor (old) man's life?" Ophelia responds, "It is the false steward that stole his master's daughter." The false steward in the "Second History" of Wotton's *Cupids Cautels* (1578) ravishes his master's daughter after making her drunk.[241] The next time we hear about Ophelia, she has drowned.

Act 4, scene 6

Since Horatio claims he came to Elsinore for old Hamlet's funeral (I.ii.), it is odd that he remains at Elsinore and curious that Hamlet knew he would still be there. Horatio now has a gentleman (Francisco), is addressed as "sir," and has immediate access to the

---

[240] In *The Arden Shakespeare "Hamlet,"* Jenkins refers to Pliny on page 456, "Pliny speaks of pouring oil of henbane in the ears (Nat. Hist., xxv.4), but he gives the result of this as mental derangement ..."

[241] Jenkins, *Arden Shakespeare "Hamlet,"* 359. Jenkins does not believe *Cupids Cautels* is a convincing source for Ophelia's story.

king.[242] Hamlet writes Horatio that he has been taken by sea pirates as their only prisoner. They treated him mercifully, "knew what they did," and Hamlet is expected to return a favor. (Was this "capture" arranged by Fortinbras?) Horatio instructs the sailors to deliver Hamlet's letters to the king and queen, then return to Horatio, so the sailors can take him to "him from whom you brought" the letters. The interim is time enough to drown Ophelia.

Q1 scene with Horatio and Gertrude

This scene is not in Q2, nor in the Folio versions.

(Horatio and the Queen)

Horatio brings Gertrude the fresh knowledge of Hamlet's return to Denmark. Horatio tells her Hamlet escaped danger and found the king's orders to have him killed upon arrival in England.

The queen responds: "Then I perceive there is treason in his looks that seem'd to sugar o'er his villainy: But I will sooth and please him for a time, for murderous mindes are always jealous ..." She asks what happened to Rosencrantz and Guildenstern. Horatio tells her that Hamlet switched the execution orders so Rosencrantz and Guildenstern were executed in place of Hamlet, and that Hamlet had his father's seal with him to seal the order.

Here, Horatio uncharacteristically shares treasonous information with someone. If it is Shakespeare's intention to show Horatio and Gertrude in close relationship, perhaps that is what is behind the ghost's persistent urging not to harm the queen.

---

[242] "In eighteenth- and nineteenth-century theatrical tradition, Horatio's companion at this point was Francisco." Thompson and Taylor, *Arden Shakespeare "Hamlet,"* 391.

Act 4, scene 7

(King and Laertes, messenger, Queen)

In this scene, it becomes known that Hamlet has returned to Denmark and that Ophelia, by drowning, has departed. With Hamlet's return, a deranged, diminished, and unpredictable Ophelia would pose an obstacle to the coup. Horatio had been asked to follow Ophelia closely and give her good watch. Who, besides "good" Horatio, could have witnessed Ophelia's drowning without attempting to save her?[243] Horatio acts quickly and dispassionately. The drowning takes place on a side-stage and punctuates the murderous discussion King Claudius has with Laertes. Francisco goes to the queen with a story of Ophelia drowning, which she then relays to the king and Laertes. Later (V.i.), the priest will describe her death as "doubtful" (suspicious).

Act 5, scene 1

(Two clowns, Hamlet, Horatio, King, Queen, Laertes, Lords attendant [including Reynaldo, Voltemand, Cornelius, and Osric], a Doctor of Divinity, the corpse)

Horatio's words are stunted in this scene. Perhaps Hamlet's remarkable return to Denmark has sobered Horatio's expectations of him. Those around Hamlet live double lives with outward appearances meshed into courtly expectations and inner agendas of self-promotion and self-preservation. He cannot trust them. No one has a relationship with Hamlet for the sake of relationship alone, except perhaps the clown

---

[243]   The question, "[W]ho could have witnessed Ophelia's drowning without attempt to save her?" is also posed in Jenkins' *Arden Shakespeare "Hamlet,"* 123.

characters. When Hamlet and Horatio come upon them (the gravedigger and his partner), Hamlet expresses surprise that the worker can sing while digging a grave. In all three texts, Horatio assures him that custom has made it in him a property of easiness. Horatio's revealing observation is not unlike Richard of Gloucester's in *Henry VI, Pt. 3*: "Why, I can smile, and murder whiles I smile, / And cry 'Content!' to that that grieves my heart, / And wet my cheeks with artificial tears, / And frame my face to all occasions. ... I'll play the orator as well as Nestor, / Deceive more slyly than Ulysses could, / And, like a Sinon, take another Troy."[244]

Hamlet picks up a discarded skull and mocks Horatio: the skull might be one "of a courtier, which could say 'Good morrow, sweet lord, how dost thou, sweet lord?' This might be Lord Such-a-one, that praised my Lord such-a-one's horse when 'a went to beg it, might it not?" To which Horatio can only parrot, "Ay, my lord." With death ("not to be") all around them, Hamlet subtly lectures Horatio for going along with the preposterous manifestation of his father's ghost. After Hamlet mentions his "lady's chamber," he says, "Horatio, tell me one thing." Horatio, hoping to avoid a direct question about Ophelia, is relieved when the question is about Alexander. But Hamlet also evaluates political ambitions: these mighty conquerors might become the dust stopping a bung-hole, or "that earth which kept the world in awe should patch a wall t' expel the water's (winter's) flaw."[245]

[244] Shakespeare, *Henry VI, Pt. 3*, Act 3, scene 2. *The Complete Works of William Shakespeare*, 560-561.

[245] "A mind that can trace Alexander's dust to a bunghole can no longer envy the heroic dedication of a Fortinbras." Robert Ornstein, from "The Moral Vision of Jacobean Tragedy" (University of Wisconsin-Madison

"Clowns" lead Hamlet to look up from his earlier "to be or not to be" dilemma (III.i.). Away from the selfish intrigues of court, he hears and perceives truths that go beyond both auspicious and inauspicious appearances of life and death. Yorick, whose bony putrefying skull can be held in Hamlet's hands, had carried child Hamlet (maybe Rosencrantz and Guildenstern, too) on his back and made him laugh. In contrast, the faked, untouchable apparition of old King Hamlet "in complete steel" (I.iv.) set Hamlet on a mission of murder. He had earlier described Fortinbras as "a delicate and tender prince whose spirit with divine ambition puffed ... [exposes] what is mortal and unsure to all that fortune, death, and danger dare, even for an eggshell" (IV.iv.). Now, with death all around him, Hamlet is repulsed by the futility of such slaughter. The bodies of great kings and fools alike turn to rotting flesh and dry bones.

Hamlet's lines, which could be building to an accusation, are interrupted by the funeral procession and his shock that the coffin holds fair Ophelia, whom he loved. At the appearance of the procession, Horatio becomes almost mute. Are spectators to believe that "friend" Horatio has had first-hand knowledge of Ophelia's madness but no lines to tell Hamlet of it? Thompson and Taylor presume Horatio has not told Hamlet about Ophelia because Horatio "supposedly left the Court to meet Hamlet at the end of 4.6. But an audience would not have time to worry about such things."[246] Yes, if spectators are not presented a more realistic, consistent, and consequential role for Horatio, they would miss considering this.

Press, 1960), reprinted in *Signet Classic Shakespeare Hamlet*, Hubler and Barnet, eds., 262.

[246] Thompson and Taylor, *Arden Shakespeare "Hamlet,"* 425.

When Laertes asks that "woe fall ten times double on that cursed head whose wicked deed" deprived Ophelia of her "most ingenious sense," though he is cursing Hamlet, spectators would turn their attention to Horatio. To close the scene, Claudius adds tension to an already charged atmosphere by asking Horatio to look after Hamlet, "I pray thee, good Horatio, wait upon him." As with Ophelia in an earlier scene, when the king puts Horatio in charge, the charge dies shortly thereafter.

Act 5, scene 2

Hamlet's enigmatic line, "So much for this, sir," leaves us wondering what "this" was. Has Horatio told him of Laertes' return and attempted attack on Claudius? What might a director use to show what Hamlet's "this" is? Next, Hamlet says, "now shall you see the other." What follows makes it clear that "the other" refers to the treacherous order he discovered on the ship to England, his clever alteration of this order, and the resultant executions of Rosencrantz and Guildenstern. Hamlet knows Horatio was in the circle of authorities when Hamlet was dispatched to England. Horatio would have entered in Act 4, scene 3, and he does not exit until after line 60 in Act 4, scene 3. Hamlet's question to Horatio, "You do remember all the circumstance?" deserves more than Horatio's equivocal reply, "Remember it, my Lord?"

Hamlet advises, "Rashly, / And praised be rashness for it — let us know / Our indiscretion sometime serves us well / When our deep plots do fall — and that should learn us / There's a divinity that shapes our ends, / Rough-hew them how we will." Horatio confesses,

"That is most certain." Hamlet's advice applies not only to the scheming deliberations of the official center stage play, but also to the underlying intrigues, where the plot to coerce the murder of Claudius grows out of control.

When Hamlet tells Horatio that Rosencrantz and Guildenstern were carrying orders that Hamlet be immediately put to death upon arrival in England, Horatio's less than compassionate, analytical reply is, "Is it possible?" At this, Hamlet gives Horatio the king's order to read at more leisure, putting a key document for the truth into the hands of Horatio. Hamlet reveals to Horatio that, "benetted round with villains" and with no leisure to overthink what he had discovered, he cunningly wrote a new commission to have Rosencrantz and Guildenstern immediately put to death—just like that, no shriving time allowed. Horatio's response is a technical, intelligence-type question about how this commission was sealed. Taken aback by this new Hamlet, he can only manage, "So Guildenstern and Rosencrantz go to 't." Hamlet replies, "They did make love to this employment" (F1), "they are not near my [Hamlet's] conscience," and "'Tis dangerous when the baser nature comes between the pass and fell incensed points of mighty opposites." Hamlet's pointed accusations about Rosencrantz and Guildenstern also describe Horatio. Since word of Hamlet's return, Horatio has already assumed a more cautious disposition toward him. Now Horatio wonders about his own safety, and what Hamlet may know about him. For Hamlet to mistakenly kill Polonius is one thing, but for him to send (likely innocent) fellow students to sudden death puts Horatio on guard.

When Horatio comments, "Why, what a King is this," Hamlet's thoughts return to Claudius. To a summary of the slings and arrows of Hamlet's outrageous fortune, and (in F1) his subsequent resolve to kill Claudius before the usurper can do more harm, Horatio again responds in intelligence-speak, telling him that a report will soon inform the king about the fate of Rosencrantz and Guildenstern.

Hamlet contemplates making things right with Laertes (F1), but this positive direction is interrupted. Osric comes to announce Claudius's wager in a duel between Laertes and Hamlet. To balance Osric's lines as the ghost in the first act, Shakespeare gives him nearly 50 lines in the last. What happens at Osric's entrance that causes Hamlet to turn to Horatio and ask if he knows him? Have Horatio and Osric appeared to recognize each other, exchanged words or looks? Does Hamlet know they know each other? Is Osric reluctant to wear the hat because he fears he will be recognized as the ghost, who always appeared with head coverings?

The play opened with a retelling of old Hamlet's duel with old Fortinbras and ends with Claudius's offer of a wager communicated through Osric. "Chivalry and honor," writes Shakespeare historian James Shapiro, "are reduced in the Danish court to jargon and an elaborate bet ..."[247] This time, Hamlet is ready. When rest and deliberation may have served him well, he chooses to let things proceed. Horatio fears (perhaps knows) the plot to kill the king will fail at the proposed duel, that Hamlet will not win, and that their positions at court will be jeopardized. He tries to stall. ("I will forestall their repair hither and say you are not fit.") Does he urge Hamlet to wait so that Fortinbras has

---

[247]   Shapiro, *A Year in the Life of William Shakespeare*, 278.

more time to arrive and storm the castle? Does he dispatch a messenger (Voltemand?) to Fortinbras?

When the court comes together for the play's final "flourish" (of three — I.ii., II.ii., and V.ii.), it balances the first one where the court gathers to hear Claudius speak of his dead brother, his kingship, his new wife, a threatening young Fortinbras, and the desires of Laertes and Hamlet to leave Elsinore to go to university. In this final act, Claudius loses both kingship and wife. Instead of pursuing distant university studies, Hamlet and Laertes die at Elsinore in a fixed wager. Fortinbras assumes the crown.

During the duel, Hamlet receives a mortal wound.[248] Facing death, Hamlet is concerned that truth will die with him, and his story remain unknown. Horatio's unhelpful response is to take the poison cup into his own hand. Has the weight of Hamlet's and other "deaths put on by cunning, and for no cause" finally crushed him, or is Horatio performing for the assembled court? If he chooses suicide, Hamlet begs him to tell their story first. In Q1, Hamlet tells Horatio to let go of the cup and reasons, "O fie Horatio, and if thou shouldst die, [w]hat a scandal wouldst thou leave behind? What tongue should tell the story of our deaths [i]f not from thee?" In Q2, Hamlet pleads with Horatio to be compassionately serious enough ("absent thee from felicity awhile") to tell Hamlet's story, even if it is painful to do so. With this plea for a just account, warlike noise is heard. Osric re-enters to explain that Fortinbras is making warlike noise at the arrival of the English ambassadors.

---

[248]   Osric exits after Hamlet cries out, "Oh Villainy! Ho! Let the door be locked. Treachery! Seek it out" (V.ii. 296-7). In *Bestrafte Brudermord*, Osric's character, Phantasmo, is in on the poisoned duel.

As Fortinbras's army breaches castle defenses, Hamlet gives his dying voice to the election of Fortinbras. (In Shakespeare's England, Robert Cecil interpreted that Queen Elizabeth's dying words and gestures determined King James VI of Scotland as her successor to the English throne.[249]) Voltemand enters with the ambassadors and Fortinbras (as in Q1). Fortinbras and Horatio address each other as if they already know each other. The English ambassador, on the other hand, uses a statelier tone and asks whom he should address. Fortinbras's "Where is this sight?" sounds as if he is responding to a message from Horatio. Horatio, already answering for the state, tells Fortinbras and the ambassadors to give order that four captains place the bodies high on a stage to view. Marcellus, Barnardo, Francisco, and the Norwegian captain place the bodies on the stage platform where the opening ghost scenes were staged.

Fortinbras's claim at the end of the play could have been James VI's claim, "For me, with sorrow I embrace my fortune. I have some right of memory in this kingdom, [w]hich now to claim my vantage doth invite me."[250] Within weeks of Elizabeth's death, James elevated Robert Cecil to Baron Cecil, of Essendon, and Cecil pronounced himself satisfied that the kingdom under James I had a promise of "greater felicity" than ever before.

Echoing the opening act, Horatio returns to oration. In front of the assembled, Horatio, whom the stage has shown to be duplicitous, declares that he will tell the yet "unknowing world [h]ow these things came about." Easily establishing authority over events,

---

[249]   Handover, *The Second Cecil*, 295-296.

[250]   One could argue, "*Hamlet* presents the possibility that the son of a foreign monarch formerly seen as an enemy [Mary Queen of Scots] could be acceptable as a king." Thompson and Taylor, *Arden Shakespeare "Hamlet,"* 40.

he will tell of "carnal, bloody and unnatural acts, of accidental judgments, casual slaughters, of deaths put on by cunning and for no cause, and purposes mistook fallen on th'inventors' heads." All this Horatio can truly deliver. Truth itself, Hamlet's dying request, will not be among the things Horatio can deliver.

Fulfilling his description in the play's opening act, Fortinbras reminds survivors that he has some rights to the kingdom and is prepared to claim them. Fortinbras is anxious to get Horatio's report out there, and these too many dead bodies cleared away so people have little chance to discover for themselves what has happened. Horatio, too, wants things settled "lest more mischance on plots and errors happen." This is consistent with Horatio's earlier warning about Ophelia, "'Twere good she were spoken with, for she may strew dangerous conjectures in ill-breeding minds" (IV.v.). Despite possible regrets and heavy collateral damage, Horatio, Fortinbras, and Osric have achieved political victories. The dead are carried off, Fortinbras claims the throne, and to the spectators' horror, Horatio owns Hamlet's story. Fortinbras gets the last words and honors Hamlet as a soldier who deserves soldier's music and the rite of war.

CONCLUSION

B efore Hamlet dies, he sadly admits, "things standing thus unknown shall live behind me" (V.ii.). His fear is not for the passing of his life, but for the lies that will live after him. He knows death will seal his lips in silence. Hamlet's plea for the living to tell what happened and his remark, "the rest is silence," are more evidence that Hamlet knows dead people do not come back to add narration to stories. That is left to the living, and even if Horatio is not trustworthy, who else could tell? Hamlet desperately asks him to give the accurate account of the events leading to Fortinbras's election.

As spectators leave the play, they imagine others who will come to Elsinore's stage to witness the tragedy of Hamlet, and "the seemingly irreversible march of the play toward its own annihilation has become what we now see as a march toward its recovery and revivification in the story of Horatio. The mortal linearity of the dramatic action will be bent by Horatio's voice into an eternal circle symbolizing the perpetuation of Hamlet's tragedy both in the memories of Shakespeare's immediate audience and in the theatres of the future."[251] I agree with Calderwood that playgoers leave knowing Horatio will tell a story of Hamlet, but I believe it will be one that protects Horatio. The real story would include Horatio's complicity in the "...

---

[251]   Calderwood, *To Be or Not to Be*, 183-184.

139

accidental judgments, casual slaughters, ... deaths put
on by cunning, and for no cause, ... purposes mistook
fallen on the inventors' heads" (V.ii.). That intrigue
brings to the play Shakespeare's genius for mistaken
identities, twisted purposes, depths of character, and
mislaid trust. At play's end, not only have spectators
seen a conspiring Horatio, but they also realize the
perpetuation of the center stage narrative has been and
will be his self-serving version of events.

The play's themes, betrayals, and some character
traits would have been recognizable in Shakespeare's
contemporaries — some tenaciously powerful and
some powerfully persecuted. Events surrounding
contemporaries (such as the Tudors, the Cecils,
Walsingham, John Dee, the Earl of Essex, Francis
Bacon, and the Stuarts), would have been close to
the playwright's mind. Perhaps *Hamlet* serves as an
alternative to the anticipated official version Francis
Bacon was ordered to create about the Essex rebellion,
or an apology for the slanderous narratives Burghley
and Walsingham created for MaryQS and others.

While writing *Hamlet*, Shakespeare may have
sympathized with historian, William Camden. A year or
two before Burghley's death in 1598, he commissioned
Camden to write the first official history of
Queen Elizabeth's reign. Camden was "deeply troubled
by this commission."[252] How much truth could be
written without upsetting his contemporaries, the most
powerful men in England, King James (MaryQS's son),
and Robert Cecil (Burghley's son and protégé)? Imagine
striking a balance that would not enrage Catholics or
Protestants. Even if Camden bravely resolved to give

---

[252] Stephen Alford, *Burghley: William Cecil at the Court of Elizabeth I* (New Haven, CT: Yale University Press, 2008), 345.

an honest account of Elizabeth's forty-five-year reign, how could he do this with torture-induced confessions, mock trials, and altered or missing state records?

Spectators are saddened at Hamlet's death and horrified that his story will be written by one who (remorselessly?) caused the deaths of so many. Horatio's plan leads to the deaths of Gertrude, Claudius, Hamlet, and any blood heir. The spectator is left to draw his own inferences from what has happened to Hamlet and what one will be told to believe about him. Then and now, spectators would consider what forces behind life-changing events are being concealed through duplicity, reckless ambition, slander, and coercion.

Some believe Shakespeare's theater presented "a deliberate threat to established authority in representing the means by which the government deployed its power and repressed opposing voices."[253] Not only does *Hamlet* "show audiences the means by which authorities wielded power and repressed opposition," the play also shows how these same authorities will create and own the narrative. Horatio's (center stage) narrative will weave story strands for surviving witnesses with strands of his invention where no survivors remain to tell a different story. He is the only major Elsinore character (with the possible exceptions of Reynaldo, Voltemand, Osric, Marcellus and Cornelius) left standing, so he probably has free license to unfold the tragedy. Horatio would do this well, at times disappearing behind his role as friend, and reducing himself to monosyllabic replies. When he would speak at length, it would be to show that he is well-informed about ghosts and politics. Public and historical events, common knowledge to occasional

---

[253] McDonald, *Bedford Companion to Shakespeare*, 318.

survivors, would be woven into Horatio's story of Hamlet. The opening dialogues with the guards, Barnardo and Marcellus, for example, would need to play out as they happened, because these two survive. Fortinbras would be King Fortinbras during the writing, so no treasonous fingers would point at him.

The play invites Shakespeare's contemporaries to avoid abusive attitudes toward illness and witchcraft, and move away from medieval superstitions and anachronisms to more natural and scientific explanations. The line between magic and religion had become blurred before the Reformation. Magic and witchcraft were still used to explain misfortune. Scot writes, "In all ages moonks and preests have abused and bewitched the world with counterfet visions … And the simple people being then so superstitious, would never seeme to mistrust [such holie men] … Now therefore let us not suffer our selves to be abused anie longer, either with conjuring preests, or melancholicall witches; but be thankfull to God that hath delivered us from such blindness and error."[254] Some of what had been perceived or controlled as supernatural could now be revealed onstage. By putting this onstage, the director guides spectators away from lingering beliefs in demons, magic, and witchcraft, while pointing out the dangers such beliefs can pose. The learned court would have had the edge on the general populace in regard to ghosts and the supernatural. They would use this edge (as Horatio does) to control people. Intelligence services, with techniques commonly used but beyond the understanding of the masses, do the same today. *Hamlet* shows us that intelligence operations can be more destructive than armor or gunpowder.

---

[254]   Scot, *Discoverie of Witchcraft*, bk. 15, chap. 39.

The play also redefines treachery and leaves us with another important lesson: survivors write the histories.[255] Yet again, the whole ear of Denmark would be rankly abused, this time by a forged process of young Hamlet's death.[256] While writing and editing his *Hamlet* in the very eventful decade straddling the turn of the century, it would have been clear to Shakespeare that survivors create history and perpetuate story lines. The play asks us to examine stories that legitimize harm and justify oppression. That Horatio will tell Hamlet's story is the most salient feature of understanding Shakespeare's intentions. A future where everything will be explained by Horatio is the deepest tragedy for the Prince of Denmark.

---

[255]   In *To Be or Not to Be*, Calderwood remarks that "what is most in danger of destruction at the end is the human voice, which is liable, as Hamlet's last words assert, to disappear in silence" (182).

[256]   Adapted from Act 1, scene 5, lines 36 to 39.

APPENDIX ONE: TIMELINE

The abbreviated "MaryQS" stands for Mary (Stuart), Queen of Scots.

1533 - Birth of Elizabeth Tudor (Elizabeth I), granddaughter of Henry VII, daughter of Henry VIII and Anne Boleyn.

1534 - Parliament renounces Papal authority and declares Henry VIII head of the Church of England.

1536 - Anne Boleyn (Elizabeth's mother) is executed.

1542 - Birth of Mary Stuart (Mary Queen of Scots), great-granddaughter of Henry VII and daughter of King James V of Scotland and Mary Guise of France.

1547 - Henry VIII dies; his son, Edward VI, becomes king.

1551 - John Dee is active in the Tudor court.

1553 - Edward VI dies. Lady Jane Grey becomes queen and is executed days later. (Catholic) Mary Tudor becomes Queen Mary I.

1557 - Scotland is proclaimed Protestant.

1558 - Mary I dies, and (Protestant) Elizabeth Tudor becomes Queen Elizabeth I. She appoints William Cecil Principal Secretary. Some consider Elizabeth illegitimate, and her cousin MaryQS the legitimate heir to the English throne.

1559–1565 - (Catholic) Mary Stuart returns to Scotland after the death of her husband, King Francis II of France. She is Queen of Scotland; marries Henry Stuart (Stewart), Lord Darnley.

1564 – Birth of William Shakespeare.

1566 - Birth of James VI, son of Mary Queen of Scots and Lord Darnley.

1567 - Lord Darnley is murdered. MaryQS marries the Earl of Bothwell. MaryQS is forced to abdicate.

1568 - MaryQS flees to England.

1568/1569–1590 - Ardently opposed to the Catholic Church, Francis Walsingham devotes himself to the queen's spy service

145

started by W. Cecil. Walsingham trains spies and double agents.

1570 - Pope excommunicates Queen Elizabeth as "the servant of infamy" and calls England "the refuge of wicked men."
- John Dee writes the preface to the English translation of Euclid's *Elements*.[257]

1571-1572 - Elizabeth elevates William Cecil to Lord Burghley.
- Elizabeth recognizes James VI as King of Scotland.
- Duke of Norfolk is executed for plotting to free MaryQS (June). - St. Bartholomew Day Massacre of Protestants in Paris (August).

1573 - Walsingham is recalled from France and named Principal Secretary.

1584 - *The Discoverie of Witchcraft*, by Reginald Scot.

1585 - Walsingham's spies identify leaders of plot seeking MaryQS's release.

1586 - Walsingham secures evidence to convict MaryQS of treason.
- *A Treatise on Melancholy*, by Timothy Bright, a protégé of Walsingham.

1587 - Walsingham brings MaryQS to trial; she is beheaded.

1588 - England defeats the Spanish Armada.

1590 - Francis Walsingham dies.

1592 - John Dee is charged with being "the conjurer of the Queen's Privy Council."[258]

1594 - Shakespeare's company first performed at court; some version of *Hamlet* is performed by his acting company. [259]

1596 - Robert Cecil succeeds his father, Lord Burghley, as Lord Chamberlain, Principal Secretary.

1597 - King James VI of Scotland (future James I of England) publishes *Daemonologie*.

1598 - Lord Burghley (William Cecil) dies.

1599 - Earl of Essex takes army to Ireland, is defeated, returns without Queen's permission and is put under house arrest.
- Printing of English histories forbidden unless sanctioned by the Privy Council.

ca. 1600 - A version of Shakespeare's *Hamlet* is performed.

---

[257] Euclid was a fourth century B.C. Greek mathematician who wrote thirteen books on geometry and other mathematics called *The Elements*.

[258] Fell Smith, *John Dee*, 294.

[259] Astington, *English Court Theatre*, 109.

1601 - Essex Rebellion fails. The day before the rebellion, Shakespeare's company performs *Richard II* for the Essex faction.
- Robert Cecil testifies at Essex's trial; Essex is sentenced to death; R. Cecil negotiates for James VI to succeed Elizabeth I.

1603 - Queen Elizabeth dies (March).
- Robert Cecil prospers under the accession of Scotland's King James to the throne of England (July).
- James becomes patron of Shakespeare's acting company renaming it The King's Men.

1603-1604 – The First Quarto and the Second Quarto texts of Shakespeare's *Hamlet* are printed.
- James adopts title, "King of Great Britain, France, and Ireland."

1616 – William Shakespeare dies.

APPENDIX TWO: SELECTED SOURCES

<u>All sources are print media except for Branagh's film, *Hamlet*,
and Johnston's lecture from the web.</u>

Aasand, Hardin L., ed. *Stage Directions in "Hamlet": New Essays
and New Directions.* Madison, NJ: Fairleigh Dickinson
University Press, 2003.

Alford, Stephen. *Burghley: William Cecil at the Court of Elizabeth I.*
New Haven, CT: Yale University Press, 2008.

Alford, Stephen. *The Watchers: A Secret History of the Reign of
Elizabeth I.* London: Penguin, 2013.

Anderson, Mark. *Shakespeare by Another Name.* New York: Gotham
Books, 2005.

Ashdown, Charles Henry. *British and Foreign Arms and Armour.*
London: T. C. and E. C. Jack, 1909.

Astington, John H. *English Court Theatre 1558-1642.* Cambridge:
Cambridge University Press, 1999.

Ball, David. *Backwards and Forwards: A Technical Manual for
Reading Plays.* Carbondale, IL: Southern Illinois
University Press, 1983.

Bede, Cuthbert. *Fotheringhay and Mary, Queen of Scots.* London:
Simpkin, Marshall, 1886.

Benedix, Roderich. *Die Shakespearomanie* (1873). In *A New Variorum
Edition of Shakespeare: Hamlet,* edited by Horace Howard
Furness, 351-354. Philadelphia: J. P. Lippincott, 1877.

Blessing, Lee. "Fortinbras," *Patient A and Other Plays.* Portsmouth,
NH: Heinemann Drama, 1995.

Blits, Jan. *Deadly Thought, Hamlet and the Human Soul.* Lanham, MD:
Lexington Books, 2001.

Bradley, A. C. *Shakespearean Tragedy: Lectures on Hamlet, Othello,
King Lear, Macbeth,* 2nd ed. London: Macmillan, 1905.

Branagh, Kenneth, director. *Hamlet.* West Hollywood: Castle Rock
Entertainment, 1996. Film.

Brewster, David. *Letters on Natural Magic, Addressed to Sir Walter Scott*. London: John Murray, 1832.

Brewster, Eleanor. *Oxford, Courtier to the Queen*. New York: Pageant Press, 1964.

Budiansky, Stephen. *Her Majesty's Spymaster*. New York: Viking Penguin, 2005.

Butler, Colin. *The Practical Shakespeare: The Plays in Practice and on the Page*. Athens, OH: Ohio University Press, 2005.

Butterworth, Philip. *Magic on the Early English Stage*. Cambridge: Cambridge University Press, 2005.

Calderwood, James L. *To Be or Not to Be: Negation and Metadrama in "Hamlet."* New York: Columbia University Press, 1983.

Camden, William. *The History of the Most Renowned and Victorious Princess Elizabeth, Late Queen of England: Selected Chapters*, edited by Wallace T. MacCaffrey. Chicago: University of Chicago Press, 1970.

Clayton, Thomas, ed. *The "Hamlet" First Published (Q1, 1603): Origins, Form, Intertextualities*. Newark, DE: University of Delaware Press, 1992.

De Groot, Hendrik. *Hamlet, Its Textual History*. Amsterdam: Swets & Zeitlinger, 1923.

Demmin, August. *Die Kriegswaffen – Ein Handbuch der Waffenkunde*. Leipzig: Seemann, 1869.

Dessen, Alan C. *Elizabethan Stage Conventions and Modern Interpreters*. Cambridge: Cambridge University Press, 1984.

Dessen, Alan C. *Recovering Shakespeare's Theatrical Vocabulary*. Cambridge: Cambridge University Press, 1995.

Dessen, Alan C. *Rescripting Shakespeare: The Text, the Director, and Modern Productions*. Cambridge: Cambridge University Press, 2002.

Dickinson, Janet. *Court Politics and The Earl of Essex, 1589-1601*. London: Pickering and Chatto, 2012.

Dillon, Janette. *The Cambridge Introduction to Early English Theatre*. Cambridge: Cambridge University Press, 2006.

Dover Wilson, John. See Wilson, John Dover.

Edge, David & John M. Paddock. *Arms & Armor of the Medieval Knight*. New York: Crown Publishers, 1988.

Eliot, T. S. "Hamlet and his Problems." *The Sacred Wood, Essays on Poetry and Criticism*. London: Methuen, 1950.

Fell Smith, Charlotte. *John Dee 1527-1608*. London: Constable, 1909.

Ffoukles, Charles. *Armour and Weapons*. Oxford: Clarendon Press, 1909.

Gajda, Alexandra. *The Earl of Essex and Late Elizabethan Political Culture*. Oxford: Oxford University Press, 2012.

Graham, Roderick. *The Life of Mary, Queen of Scots: An Accidental Tragedy*. New York: Pegasus, 2009.

Greg, W. W. "Hamlet's Hallucination." *The Modern Language Review* 12, no. 4 (Oct 1917): 393-421.

Guy, John A. *Queen of Scots: The True Life of Mary Stuart*. Boston: Houghton Mifflin, 2004.

Hall, Bert S. *Weapons and Warfare in Renaissance Europe*. Baltimore: Johns Hopkins University Press, 1997.

Handover, P. M. *The Second Cecil: The Rise of Power 1563-1604 of Sir Robert Cecil, later Earl of Salisbury*. London: Eyre & Spottiswoode, 1959.

Haynes, Alan. *Invisible Power: The Elizabethan Secret Services, (1570-1603)*. New York: St. Martin's Press, 1992.

Haynes, Alan. *Robert Cecil, 1st Earl of Salisbury*. London: Peter Owen Publishers, 1989.

Hayter, Alethea. *Horatio's Version*. London: Faber and Faber, 1972.

Heppenstall, Rayner and Michael Innes. *Three Tales of Hamlet*, pages 75-89. London: Gollancz, 1950.

Hewlett, Maurice Henry. *The Queen's Quair or The Six Years' Tragedy*. New York: Scribner's, 1912.

Honigmann, E. A. J. *Myriad-Minded Shakespeare: Essays, Chiefly on the Tragedies and Problem Comedies*, 2nd ed. New York: St. Martin's Press, 1998.

Hubler, Edward and Sylvan Barnet, eds. *The Tragedy of Hamlet, Prince of Denmark* by William Shakespeare. New York: Signet Classics, Penguin, 1987.

Ioppolo, Grace. *Revising Shakespeare*. Cambridge, MA: Harvard University Press, 1992.

Jenkins, Harold, ed. *The Arden Shakespeare "Hamlet,"* 2nd series. London: Methuen, 1982.

Johnston, Ian, "Introductory Lecture on Shakespeare's *Hamlet*." www.mala.bc.ca/~Johnstoi/eng366/lectures/hamlet. htm 2001, 27 Feb. 2001. (accessed May 2, 2008).

Kinney, Arthur F., ed. *"Hamlet": New Critical Essays*. New York: Routledge, 2002.

Kliman, Bernice W., and Paul Bertram, eds. *The Three-Text Hamlet: Parallel Texts of the First and Second Quartos and First Folio*, 2nd ed. New York: AMS Press, 2003.

Knight, Charles, ed. *Shakspere, a Biography*. London: C. Knight & Co., 1843.

Knight, Charles, ed. *The Pictorial Edition of the Works of Shakspere*. New York: P. F. Collier, 1893.

Knight, Charles, ed. *The Pictorial Edition of the Works of Shakspere, Tragedies*, vol. 1. New York: P. F. Collier, 1851.

Knight, Charles, ed. *The Pictorial Edition of the Works of Shakspere, Tragedies*, vol. 1. London: C. Knight & Co., 1843.

Knight, Charles, ed. *The Pictorial Edition of the Works of Shakspere, the Histories*, vol. 1. London: Routledge, 1867.

Lacey, Robert. *Robert, Earl of Essex: An Elizabethan Icarus*. London: Weidenfeld and Nicolson, 1971.

Laking, Guy Francis. *Catalogue of the European Armour and Arms in the Wallace Collection at Hertford House*. London: His Majesty's Stationery Office, 1901.

Levi, Peter. *Horace: A Life*. London: Duckworth & Co., 1997.

Marshall, Rosalind K. *Elizabeth I*. Owings Mills, MD: Stemmer, 1991.

Mason, H. A. "The Ghost in *Hamlet*, A Resurrected 'Paper.'" *Cambridge Quarterly* III, no. 2 (1967-8): 127-152.

McDonald, Russ. *The Bedford Companion to Shakespeare*. Boston: Bedford Books, 1996.

Moorman, F. W. "The Pre-Shakespearean Ghost." *Modern Language Review* 1, no. 6 (1905): 85-95.

Moorman, F. W. "Shakespeare's Ghosts." *Modern Language Review* 1, no. 6 (1905): 192-201.

Norman, A. V. B. and Don Pottinger. *A History of War and Weapons (449-1660)*. New York: Thomas Y. Crowell, 1966.

Oakshott, R. *A Knight and His Armour*. London: Camelot Press, 1961.

Orgel, Stephen. *The Authentic Shakespeare, and Other Problems of the Early Modern Stage*. New York: Routledge, 2002.

Orgel, Stephen. *The Illusion of Power: Political Theater in the English Renaissance*. Los Angeles: UC Berkeley Press, 1975.

Pearson, Daphne. *Edward de Vere (1550-1604): The Crisis and Consequences of Wardship*. London: Ashgate, 2005.

Pfaffenbichler, Matthias. *Armourers (Medieval Craftsmen Series)*. Toronto: University of Toronto Press, 1992.

Planché, James Robinson. *Cyclopedia of Costume*. London: Clowes and Sons, 1876.

Planché, James Robinson. *History of British Costume*, New Edition. London: C. Cox and Clowes and Sons, 1847.

Prosser, Eleanor. *Hamlet and Revenge*. Stanford, CA: Stanford University Press, 1967.

Quetel, Claude. *History of Syphilis* (1986), translated by Judith Braddock and Brian Pike. Baltimore: Johns Hopkins University Press, 1992.

Rice, Robert Spring. *The Story of Hamlet and Horatio*. London: Selwyn, 1924.

Richmond, Velma Bourgeois. *Shakespeare, Catholicism, and Romance*. New York: Continuum International, 2000.

Ronald, Susan. *Heretic Queen: Queen Elizabeth I and the Wars of Religion*. New York: St. Martin's Press, 2012.

Scofield, Martin. *The Ghosts of Hamlet: The Play and Modern Writers*. Cambridge: Cambridge University Press, 1980.

Scot, Reginald. *The Discoverie of Witchcraft*. London: William Brome, 1584. Republished with an introduction by Montague Summers. London: J. Rodker, 1930.

Shakespeare, William. *The Complete Works of William Shakespeare*. Masters Library ser. London: Octopus Books; Minneapolis: Amaranth, 1985.

Shapiro, James. *A Year in the Life of William Shakespeare: 1599*. New York: Harper Perennial, 2006.

Sider Jost, Jacob. "*Hamlet's* Horatio as an Allusion to Horace's *Odes*." *Notes and Queries* 59, no. 1 (2012): 76-77.

Smith, Charlotte Fell. See Fell Smith, Charlotte.

Smith, Lacey Baldwin. *Treason in Tudor England, Politics and Paranoia*. Princeton, NJ: Princeton University Press, 1986.

Spurgeon, Caroline F. E. *Shakespeare's Imagery and What It Tells Us*. Cambridge: Cambridge University Press, 1935.

Strype, John. *The Annals of the Reformation and Establishment of Religion, and Other Various Occurrences in the Church of England, during Queen Elizabeth's Happy Reign: Together with an Appendix*, vol. 3, pt. 2. Oxford: Clarendon Press, 1824.

Thompson, Ann and Neil Taylor, eds. *The Arden Shakespeare "Hamlet,"* 3rd ser., London: Thomson Learning, 2007.

Thompson, Ann and Neil Taylor, eds. *The Arden Shakespeare "Hamlet,"* 3rd ser., Rev. ed., London: Bloomsbury Arden Shakespeare, 2016.

Virgil. *Aeneid*, translated by Robert Fagles. London: Penguin, 2006.

Warley, Christopher. "Specters of Horatio." *ELH* 75, no. 4 (2008): 1023-1050.

Weir, Alison. *Mary, Queen of Scots, and the Murder of Lord Darnley.* New York: Ballantine Books, 2009.

Wilson, John Dover. *The Essential Shakespeare.* Cambridge: Cambridge University Press, 1932.

Wilson, John Dover. *What Happens in "Hamlet,"* 3rd ed. Cambridge: Cambridge University Press, 1951.

Wilson, John Dover, ed. *The Tragedy of Hamlet, Prince of Denmark.* 2nd ed. Cambridge: Cambridge University Press, 1936, rev. 1954.

Wright, Iain. "'Come like shadowes, so depart': The Ghostly Kings in *Macbeth.*" *The Shakespearean International Yearbook* 6 (October 2006): 215-229.

Wright, Iain. "All Done with Mirrors: Macbeth's Dagger Discovered." *HEAT* 10, new series (November 2005): 179-200.

CPSIA information can be obtained
at www.ICGtesting.com
Printed in the USA
LVHW080032121219
640222LV00018B/1387/P

9 781495 810759